WHITE HORSE FORCE

WHO CAN MAKE ME A
SUPER-IMMORTAL?

M.A. Meehan

PRESS

Look For The Sequel In 2015/2016
WHITE HORSE FORCE: Book Two
"How Can I Rule the Future?"

DEDICATION

To the Holy Spirit. . .
Who never ceases to surprise me!

INTRODUCTION

Want to enjoy a supernatural reality show? Want to get a glimpse of the REAL post-apocalyptic Earth? Want to find out how you can (literally) rise above it as a super-immortal?

Rule number one is "know your enemy." But what if you do not know you are in a war? And what if the enemy is invisible?

The force that motivates terrorists cannot be overcome by Superman, Batman, Spiderman Iron Man or Wonder Woman!

Only the Cosmic Commander with a White Horse Force of millions of super-immortals riding out of the sky can evict it and impose world peace.

Do you want to join? This celestial citizenship is to die for…even more than chocolate and vampires!

FLY WITH THE MOST HIGH

CONTENTS

_ᑶᑾ_

WHITE HORSE FORCE:
BOOK ONE

WHO CAN MAKE ME A *SUPER-IMMORTAL?*

PART ONE

ANGEL WARS:
THE STORY OF YOUR ENEMY

1
Evil is Birthed in Heaven

Long ago, far beyond all galaxies, a celestial creature stared at his flashing, jeweled garments. At the control center of the universe, the blinding brilliance of his beauty was awesome. Why shouldn't he admire himself? Wasn't he called Lucifer, Light-Bearer, Daystar? Wasn't he the highest ranking, supreme musician, worship leader and guardian of the throne of the Most High? [1]

Looking down at the dazzling, multi-colored gems in gold-settings covering his "suit of lights," pride began to enter his heart. Walking back and forth on the "stones of fire," he started to meditate on his future. "Have I not been given perfect wisdom? What other archangel is clothed in every precious stone; diamond, topaz, sapphire, emerald, turquoise, onyx? Why shouldn't I be a king and have a throne on the new, special planet I've heard will be created?"[2]

But as he glanced up at the magnificent divine fire of the Most High, his face twisted into a mask of mingled envy, arrogance and rebellion. At this point, evil was conceived for the first time. Original sin was planned and plotted. Not on Earth which was yet to be created, but right in the power headquarters of heaven. But would it succeed? How could it happen so close to the Creator? Could high treason, anarchy, civil war even appeal to the angels? Would angel wars now begin? If so, when and where and how could they possibly end?

As intrigue began to balloon in his brain, Lucifer soared through the galaxies with new speed. It was all so unique and radical. Unheard of really. Who would have dreamed such a thought could be born in the supernatural mind of the highest servant of the Divine Majesty.

Excitement began to tingle through his body until it reached a kind of perverse ecstasy. He would be the first, the only, the greatest opponent; the inventor of opposition to the exclusive claims of the Most High. On the other hand, what if he failed? What if none of the lower angels would follow his leadership into a new kingdom? Suppose he couldn't find any who would challenge their Creator? How would he deal with that?

But just as these doubts darkened his thoughts, a sudden flash of insight lit up his laser-like eyes. Of course! None of the angels would join his revolution unless he had bait! But what could he offer them that they didn't already have in their perfect celestial sphere? POWER! That was it! When his new opposing kingdom was formed, he would promise them positions as princes[3] and rulers over the various lands of the creatures the Most High would put on his first plant...Earth. It would be an offer they couldn't refuse. A fool proof plan. Now, all that was needed was a manifesto – a declaration and proclamation of his future victory. That would convince even the lowest angelic servant for the need of another, alternate kingdom which, after all, would be only what Lucifer's glorious and exalted position deserved!

Distant future visions and fantasies began to crowd his consciousness. He saw himself appearing as an angel of light on the planet Earth; beguiling, enticing, seducing and deceiving the future race of God's creatures there. Then morphing into a dragon, he saw billions of them bowing in fear and terror before his image. As he manipulated and blinded their minds, he saw vast multitudes of Earth dwellers reject the love of the Most High and even deny that He had created them.

Now convinced it would all really happen as he had imagined, uncontrollable laughter shook him. It was going to be great fun to see them grovel and fall for his kingdom of darkness unaware! He would be their only light, the great, invincible Lucifer, their only god and master!! Finally, the Most High would have some competition. Why shouldn't there be choices? Why should there be only one God? Independence

17

and freedom would be great concepts to promote, even a possible slogan for recruitment into his kingdom.

As he now prepared to write his manifesto, another idea emerged in his rapidly hardening heart. Why write it at all? Hadn't the Godhead simply spoke everything into existence out of nothing? Why couldn't just speaking work for him, too? But after a chill rattled his being, he decided just to say it in his heart, and not speak out loud since he was still close to the Throne Room.

Perplexed by his still lingering fears of the Most High, he decided that if his plan didn't materialize, he would write it down later. Perhaps it would be called "the eternal scroll of Lucifer" or something even better than that! "Celebrate!" This called for the fun of freedom to begin! A secret celestial party, hidden from the Most High! Also, the first Luciferian summit conference to lure his army of first time rebels...to be recorded as the greatest innovation ever conceived.

Envisioning the impact of this announcement, his beautiful face suddenly turned hideously fierce. A major personality change would now be in order. As commander of the first war in eternity, he couldn't indulge anyone with that love, kindness and mercy valued by the Most High. He did, however, consider the wisdom of using it as bait to gain the dumb Earthlings' trust.

NO, his style of rule would definitely be different. What about creative ways to say the opposite of everything the Creator would say? Perhaps a new invention of reverse thought? A name would be needed for it. LIES! Whether big ones or small ones, if they could be repeated continually, over and over and over for generations, many would believe them as fact. In the end, they wouldn't be able to tell the difference between lies and truth, or good and evil. Confusion would triumph! They would call good evil and evil good! Wow! What a thrill! Then the subversion of his new role as a Satan would be a smashing success.

He could see it all now. This system would be unstoppable and spread like wildfire! He would call it MAGIC! But first, before summoning his fellow angels with his exhilarating music, he decided to scream out his manifesto inside his brain. Although not audible in the atmosphere it reverberated all the way to the throne of the Most High Power.

> "I will ascend to heaven. I will raise my throne
> above the stars of God. I will sit enthroned on
> the mount of assembly, on the utmost heights
> of the sacred mountain. I will ascend above
> the tops of the clouds. I will make myself like
> the Most High."

There. It was done. An absolute first! No one else had ever dared to dream of such a thing. But he, the unique Lucifer, would be the only one to achieve it. Now, grinning, laughing, frowning, and writhing in grotesque contortions all at the same time, he congratulated himself on his superior intelligence. Since he would be doing the seemingly impossible how could the lower angels not admire his scheme?

Composing himself and straightening up into his regal posture, Lucifer flew to the appointed place of meeting...the Daystar. It was his personal namesake light source! He was amazed when, out of shock and curiosity, one third of the angels actually showed up. Then, hearing his offer of new royalty and exalted powers, they never went back!

Intense excitement rippled through the assembly of celestial beings. Yes! They would conquer! Why not? Weren't there millions more of them than the three person Godhead? Having heard the rumor about the new, tiny experimental planet, they would wait and help Lucifer establish his rival god status there. Of course if they had stopped to think about it, they all would have remembered that God could monitor their secret plans and knew everything they did (and said) before they did it. Nevertheless, it was too late to back out now. Jumping at the chance for a change, they really hadn't considered the consequences.

2
COSMIC WAR IS DECLARED

Lucifer was so convincing, and his new authority mode was overwhelming. All of a sudden, shouting and screeching erupted from millions of angels' mouths. Defiance, cursing, insults and hatred were hurled at the Most High Power. Now, boldly declaring themselves to be His first and only enemies, they danced a new dance–a gyrating, writhing, twisting travesty of their former holy dance. Shuddering at the vortex of a pit looming in the distance, they all bowed to their new lord and king–trapped forever in his compelling service.

A great declaration was made. They would worship only him and fight only for his kingdom. Using any tactics, any devices, they would become gods and goddesses by his supreme power. And he would become the great Adversary, Satan, waging eternal war against his Creator and all creatures loyal to Him. But, meanwhile, what about the angels who had decided to remain loyal to Yahweh Elohim–the name of the creator God?

Grieving at the defection and treason of so many of their companions, they had rushed for comfort to the great angel prince Michael, who assured them of his own loyalty and certain victory in the end. Indeed, he had already heard there would be a final battle between himself and Satan, with the outcome pre-determined by the most High.

As the holy angels were weeping for the loss of their former friends and co-workers, Michael told them that he had heard a future prophet would even be asked to lament[4] for Lucifer! However, right now God was about to answer the five "I wills" of his manifesto. "Yet you will be cast down to the pit."[5] Was that it? Was that to be the only punishment for a career of untold terror, horror and destruction? Not exactly.

In the heart of the Godhead, fury was rising at the foreseen atrocities of Satan and an unthinkable place was being prepared for him and his angels. Meanwhile, at the council of the Most High, shock, panic and outrage were not evident, far from it. Knowing all things in advance from beginning to end, Elohim couldn't ever be mystified or surprised at anything. Yet their emotions were always stirred by what did happen.

Although long aware of what Lucifer would do, they still couldn't help feeling sad when he did it. Maybe they shouldn't have even created him to begin with, realizing how he would turn out. Or perhaps he and his army should be exiled and locked up immediately.

But no, Elohim would not ignore their challenge. They had defied the Living God and He would now allow their evil to run full course while keeping Lucifer on a long leash. He could utilize his schemes to bring about good. In reality, this enemy outburst had already been programmed into their vast eternal plan.

But still, a tragic number of angels had just failed the test. Though God knew the great risk in making creatures with free will, how else could love and loyalty have meaning? Certainly not from mindless robots who had no choice. Being romantic, the Father, Son and Spirit all craved love and intimate friendship. Being infinite themselves, they wanted an immense extended family to lavish rewards and pleasures on forever. In fact, God would say later in His Book that He created everything for His pleasure![6]

Now, His ultimate masterpiece was about to appear; a very tiny jewel of a planet to be unique in the universe. Despite the recent angel upheaval, the time arrived for the incredible experiment. A totally new planet, astoundingly beautiful...even an amazing reflection of heaven itself. Because it would contain features and creatures found nowhere else in the universe, a special environment had to be created to maintain life. Watching all this work emerge out of nothing, the holy angels sang for joy...but Satan was plotting his takeover.

Lucifer's angels shuddered. Moaning, screeching and gasping they could hardly believe what they heard. As the great wheels of fire propelled the emerald rainbow throne across the pavement of sapphire, the thunderous, water-fall voice of the Most High boomed out their fate. "For the unheard of abominations you will commit, I am preparing chains of darkness, an abyss, and even a lake of non-con-suming, eternal fire for you, Satan, and your angels. You will become the devil and they will become demons enslaved in your doomed kingdom. Those beings I am creating on My new planet, Earth, will fear and tremble at your power as you steal, kill and destroy; they will forget about Me. Their love will grow cold turning into the delusion of pride and they will become fools headed for the same lake of forever fire."[7]

Knowing that the law of the angels allowed no second chance, they were now unable to change their minds and return to the presence of Divine Love again. For all eternity, they were locked into this strange new mindset. Gradually, an unusual feeling began to rise up inside them. Starting to feel a sort of rage spreading to the very core of their con-sciousness, it was frightening and thrilling at the same time. A nameless, all consuming passion gripped them. A new mind-numbing thing was blocking out all their original heav-enly behavior patterns. Feeling like a firestorm against every desire of their Creator, it would come to be called HATE!

Trembling and leaping, they shot up millions of arms with fists raised toward the fiery throne. Yes! Yes! Yes! They would fight the holy angels forever. They would form ranks in the first celestial army of Lucifer. They would be invincible! They would proclaim the power of hate even by disguises of love. They were elated and exhilarated.

But now, Satan was slowly beginning to see the problem. What if this new emotion of hate spread among his own servants? How could his army be unified in its assault if constant infighting and malice made them attack each other?[8] Quickly, he realized the only solution would be a rigid, ironclad hierarchy. Ruling princes would be appointed to keep the underlings in line. These would be control spirits, keeping order by threats, fear and brute force. Underlings could only vent their fury on Earth creatures, enticing them into attractive traps. Entertainment would be their specialty.

Lucifer laughed when it dawned on him that none of his devices could surpass his invention of propaganda. Wouldn't efficiency increase if he formulated a system of mega-lies? Why not continually bombard his troops with the opposite of truth? Only the enemy Elohim knew what that was anyway. Perhaps all that was needed was to repeat continually: "We will win! We will conquer the Most High. We will replace God. We will rule heaven and Earth forever and ever. There is no abyss, there is no lake of fire. God is a liar."

Somehow, he knew it would work. Words were dynamite packages of power. Hadn't even God created everything out of nothing by His words? Wasn't His Son even called "The Word of God?" So how could he fail? Yes, he too would prevail with words!

Lucifer could hardly believe his ears. Could it be his request had been granted? Even by his infinite Enemy? But, yes, it had really happened. His joy was full! A decree had gone forth from the Most High Throne granting him access for a temporary assignment to the new mini-planet. Hardly containing his excitement, he blared forth vibrating, deafening music to trumpet the news of his own domain at last. But his happiness was to be brief.

Immediately afterward, it was announced that, at a set time, (for time would exist only on Earth), the Son of The Most High Himself would also visit the planet, disguised as an Earth dweller! There were even rumors He would secretly form a future white horse force to take over Satan's dominion. Well, he couldn't think about this preposterous idea now. Never had he imagined such absurd foolishness would occur to the Great Godhead. Better just to ignore it!

In any case, if anyone ever asked, his strategy would be to deny it...relentlessly deny it. In fact, denial of all pronouncements and promises of the Most High would be his most deadly weapon. Yes, continual, deadly denial!

3
THE KINGDOM OF DARKNESS FORMS

_Cͻ cͻ_

Constant rejection would wipe out the agenda of his Adversary from the brains of Earthlings. He might even call it "brainwashing!" Wouldn't they then know that nothing the Most High said could be believed? This would take work, of course, for him to unleash his greatest powers of intimidation, mocking, scoffing, and ridicule. But naturally, or rather supernaturally, he also knew that the hearts of these so-called humans weren't going to endure being empty. Something would have to be done about that!

As the idea started coming to him, Lucifer's face glowed again with some of its lost light. It would be a masterpiece! Who could exceed his versatility? He has something for everyone! He is all things to all people! Diversity University! Tolerance of anything except God's literal words. Seductive snares and soul slavery would be subtle and beautiful. If they liked opulent pageantry and ceremony, he would give them that. If they liked simple, plain austerity, he would give them that. If they liked nature worship, wizards and idols, he would certainly oblige. Whatever seemed to work, whether scientific mind games, gross abuse orgies or goddess apparitions, he would help them to be happily deceived.

Lawlessness would be labeled liberation or religion, depending on the case. On the other hand, great expert leaders could exalt themselves to impose systems of detailed rituals so complex that the burdened underlings would end up hopeless. Bondage of spirit and soul would be the goal… not to mention a good way to get rich! Extortion by fear would be the sure way to wealth. Whatever it took, he, Lucifer, would lure as many as possible to share his future in the lake of fire! But no matter what, never let them know how to get to heaven.

Hearing about this, Satan's angels were getting excited. The potential of building his kingdom was assured. Plans for making fools were foolproof! Anxious to get started right away, they began testing torture techniques on each other. "Hold it," said Satan, "not so fast. We haven't finished the fine points of our formula yet."

Then, directing them to choose their specialties, he told his new ruling princes to keep order. Auditions would be held for seducers, teachers, tormentors, familiar impersonators, mind blinded guides, liars, and haunters. However, the most special attention was to be given to a whole range of appearances delightful to children. It was rumored that the Most High would give these human creatures the unheard of power to multiply! Their little offspring would be called children and be most susceptible to supernatural influence. For them, inventions of tiny, amusing beings to be called Fairies, Elves, Trolls, Leprechauns, and Goblins would be just the thing to captivate them at an early age. Then, because they would be such fun, nobody would pay attention to what ideas they were teaching. Public outrage would be heaped on any who dared criticize or expose these beloved little entertainers. Figuring that Earth dwellers would not like to think for themselves, Satan knew his spiritual spider webs would trap most of them. That thought was to give him the only comfort he could get from now on.

Feeling good about the structure of his kingdom so far, a flash of insight hit him that inflated his pride to the next level. What about telling Earthlings that his, Lucifer's, dream could be theirs? They could become like God! If they would just look inside themselves, and work to become "enlightened" by rituals he would devise, they could realize they were God. The only catch here was that everyone else would also be God...along with everything else in the cosmos. But, not to worry, because the goal of it all would be "Nirvana" or total annihilation. So, who would know the difference then anyway? A perfect plan, if he did say so himself (and he usually did)! This way, the whole concept of Yahweh's

Truth would flip-flop into reverse! Nothingness would be more fascinating than heaven! Merging mindlessly with the universe would cancel all rewards and punishments. Better to recycle into numerous next lives and improve "Karma" on Earth.

If complicated religions wouldn't be enough to totally confuse humankind, Lucifer decided he might have to invent something called "Psychology" as his specialty. As a showcase for his ancient wisdom, he knew it would outwit Earthlings at every turn. Now ecstatic at the way his plans were going, he realized that the so called icing on the cake (Devil's Food, of course), would be to prevent anyone knowing that God wanted a personal relationship with them.

If he had his way, never would any religious system hint at such a thing. Nobody would know that interactive friendship could be possible. If they ever asked, his demons would be quick to rebuke with, "Oh, you think you can have a pipeline to God?" No, God's love would have to be kept at a vast distance. Better to keep it in the abstract. Maybe only as a theory that nobody would know how to experience. Then he, Satan, could appear as an angel of light (his former self) and provide a great counterfeit!

However, it was always depressing to remember that the Most High knew all about this and has a countering plan out there somewhere. Often, he wondered and worried what it could be. He hoped to get a clue before it actually happened. Still, he was mystified about why God would want to make this new race of Earth creatures. Weren't the angels, His personally crafted messengers and worshippers, enough to satisfy all the desires of the Most High? Even the two thirds of them left loyal to His kingdom should be plenty to find pleasure in.

What could be the point of a microscopic planet full of new, weird life forms? Questions flooded Lucifer's heart (what was left of it), and a chilling premonition of danger dawned. He couldn't put his finger on it, but somehow there was something ominous about what was to be his home away from home. He had a distinctly sinister sensation of a trap awaiting him on their soil.

But brushing aside such caution, he quickly returned to revel in his favorite fantasies. Glancing down at his bejeweled body armor, he was confident that no Earthling could be created to compare with his own magnificence. Lives of the rich and famous would be laughable in the light of his! He would dazzle them all with exquisite supernatural splendor undreamed of.

His army was now meeting frequently and secretly to plan kingdom of darkness operations. Since not all angels had been created with the same level of intelligence or power, the stronger were keeping the simpletons in line. As Satan officially installed his hierarchy of principalities, powers and rulers of wickedness in high places, shouts of "Hail Lucifer" thundered through the crowd. But among the mighty cheers there were also fears of a possible reprisal from the still dreaded Godhead. However, all that would have to change when their glorious commander took control. Then the Most High would have to move over and share His throne with Satan.

4
MASTER LIARS
OF THE UNIVERSE

S o why not go for the gold? (Or rather the fire,[9] which was what surrounded God's throne.) After all, he had nothing to lose. He couldn't go back. There was no second chance, no forgiveness for angels. They knew too much. Turning aside a twinge of remorse, Lucifer laughed at the fun he was going to have manipulating these mere mortals on their mini-mud ball of a planet. Wouldn't he prove that they couldn't be any more loyal to the Most High than the angels?

Just as he finished congratulating himself and his princes on the future of these plans, a new idea struck him with such force that he knew it was the most hideous, hilarious masterpiece of all! "I'll deny that I even exist! Deny that there is any supernatural at all! Deny there is a God who ever did anything or will do anything! Deny anything unseen exists (especially me)! Deny God wants to make personal contact! Deny God is a Person! Deny that He even exists! Yes! Yes! Yes! Deny is the perfect lie! No need to prove the point! Just deny, deny, deny! Intimidate and lie!"

Leering and sneering, Lucifer cackled, "We'll see what the Most High could ever come up with to combat the irresistible popularity of this! Everybody is sure to love it because humans won't have to hope for anything called Truth. I think I'll even call it "Humanism"! And since by that time they'll all be their own gods, they won't fear anything but public opinion. It will be government "of the gods, by the gods and for the gods!" All this time, Satan's new princes of darkness had been listening and learning well. Now, one of their top evil geniuses shouted for permission to speak. In a clear, cool, precise manner, he pointed out that while his Excellency, the Dragon King's denial system was brilliant, perhaps another replacement doctrine might be in order. In fact, all kinds of replacement doctrine might be in order. All kinds of replacements could work better than pure denial! The actual flip side of the coin of DENY would be REPLACE!

"Of course! Of course!!" Lucifer was delirious! "Why didn't I see that myself? Oh, well, I can't think of everything... that's what my ruling class will be for." At this, all of his kingdom creatures who were designated rulers of darkness, began flying up and down with great excitement. It had to be admitted that some of them were coming up with excellent ideas. For instance, when it would be continually denied that the Most High created the new planet and everything in it, they would be ready with a great replacement. In a short time, it would be easy to just convince the Earthlings that they developed ever so slowly from nothing at all (or maybe pond scum), and over a very vast span of time, gradually changed from other animals into so-called humans. Then, convinced it took them so much time to emerge, they'll feel cut off from any mental or spiritual connection to God. Those few who refuse this scenario will be intimidated by labels of "religious fanatic"! After this presentation, shouts of "Bravo" went up all around. Clearly, denial and replacement of Creation would ensure victory for their kingdom.

But perhaps even that might not be enough to cover everything. Above and beyond Creation there was one last issue that, if overlooked, could wipe out everything they worked for. Finally, it struck them all that the #1 most important denial must be all ideas of God ever ruling on Earth! No matter what else happens, the Kingdom of God must never, never, ever, come down out of the heavens and actually take over from Satan and his angels.

Lucifer was livid at the mere mention of any such concept. "It must be stamped out at all costs," he fumed. "I'll just keep repeating over and over and over, until the whole Earth is saturated, that the Kingdom of God is ONLY spiritual...

ONLY unseen and ONLY on the INSIDE of humans!" Hearing this, the dragon angels all clapped and cheered!

"We'll see to it, won't we, that great tolerance must be enforced at all times for the diversity of religions I'm going to create. I think I'll call them 'Faith Traditions'! And now hear this. This is paramount! Whatever place the Most High might ever announce as reserved for His future throne on Earth, that spot must be destroyed! If it takes every strategy of our superior intelligence, we must constantly struggle against whatever nation and people might try to hold this land for Him. Even if it takes every army on Earth, we will conquer. We will rule forever!

"No matter what it takes, we will always stop God from putting His King and His army on the Earth! No huge number of victims and martyrs could be too great to sacrifice for the glory of me – the eternal Dragon King! This denial is our major priority!

"A relentless campaign must be launched at the earliest opportunity. Never will it be too soon to start getting the word out that NO PLACE on Earth will ever have any special significance to God. All places and lands are the same to Him! And if any group should start teaching that He would sit down on a throne to rule from one certain Earth city, this must always be denounced as the bizarre delusion of a few fringe fanatics. But why should I worry? Don't I know I can trust my seducing spirits and teaching demons to keep the majority in line? Their mind-blinding techniques will accomplish it!

"That will put the non-conformists in their place, and if any still disagree, well, THEY will have to be REPLACED! Any land on Earth, however tiny, that God might be rash enough to claim for His future headquarters, will have to be challenged, denounced, harassed and invaded non-stop. Any king there claiming to be God would have to be killed, just in case."

Finally, the planning stages were over. Ah, what masteries and mysteries were hatched in the hallowed halls of heaven! From grotesque to gorgeous, their cosmic bag of tricks would never be surpassed. NEVER! Now, as Creation Week loomed on the horizons of space, the angel army of wickedness would fly forth chanting their slogan "DEATH TO HUMANS!!!"

Aware of the cosmic battle brewing, suspense was building between the two angel armies. While the loyalists headed by Michael were double the number of Lucifer's rebels, they were restricted by tactics of only goodness, love and justice. No lie would be permitted to cross their lips. But, after all, didn't they have the Most High on their side? In the end, their King would bring total victory along with a mysterious white horse force they had heard rumors about. Whenever that would happen, they would get to fly alongside!

Knowing that nothing could ever be a dilemma for the Almighty, they would be His faithful messengers zooming through space like stars or flames of fire. So, despite the fight they faced with the traitor angels, they remained calm and joyful, singing God's praises in great lyric beauty at the Holy center of His throne. Adoration mounted into exaltation as the blinding Eternal Light called the Sun Of Righteousness glowed out toward them in beams of radiant love! Would He ever go down personally, they wondered, to shine His love light on the tiny planet He was about to form? So many questions crowded their minds that it was all they could do to keep from blurting them out.

What scary, horrendous things were coming when the now two kingdoms clashed on the future battleground called Earth? But, far from joining in the praise and worship of which he had once been the conductor, Satan sulked. Out of nowhere, he was seized with violent shaking and trembling. A deep depression hit him with the impact of the abyss. What had he done? The love of God was utterly lost forever! Eternal separation! Waves of icy chills gripped the empty edges of his soul, and the baggage of death began to move in.

Little did he dream that even Yahweh Elohim had wept at his unchangeable choice. Not only that, but thousands of Earth years later, God would even direct one of His trusted prophets to write a lament for Lucifer when he would be the power behind a future world trade throne.[10]

WHITE HORSE FORCE:
Book One

Who Can Make Me a *Super-Immortal?*

PART TWO

LOVE'S LABORATORY:
The Story of Your Planet

5
SEXTACY IN EDEN

⏤᷒⏤

Finally, the great Creation Week had arrived. Six evenings and mornings followed by a day off! When they saw it, all the angels sang together.[11] Some sang for a different reason, with their hidden agenda. Hardly hiding his contempt for the angels who refused to join him, Lucifer decided to concentrate on subverting humans to replace them.

As the two groups of angels monitored Earth's emergence in space, each believed that their kingdom would triumph in time. Time, of course, was a whole new concept none of the angels knew anything about, but the idea had already leaked out somehow. It was thought to be some sort of restriction used to keep order. But what was the mysterious new emotion called "hope" which was supposed to be connected to it?

Not wanting to ask, the loyal angels decided to take a wait-and-see attitude. What they had already been told, however, was that each of them would be given an Earth person to protect, usually in secret. Especially, they would be assigned to watch over the littlest ones, but also the bigger ones on reserve for God's kingdom. Why would these humans need to have Divine protection? No need to ask. It was most obvious to all the holy angels who had watched with horror the revolt of Lucifer and his duped defectors!

But now it was really happening: The creation of the first planet[12] out of absolutely nothing. Later, the spiraling galaxies of sparkling stars would make it look surprisingly small. A blue-green swirled planet, like a little gem stone, it had a certain hint of heaven about it!

Zooming down for a closer look, they heard the voice of the Almighty booming like a waterfall: "Let there be light!" No sooner said than it happened! The Light Of The World rushed to the scene, creating everything precisely as His Father spoke it. Not until the fourth day would a much less intense light be made especially for the Earth. Also, as a night light, a soft, glowing pearl of a planet was formed. This sun and moon were to have a great importance in the whole panorama of the coming Earth drama!

But, why, wondered the angels, was He forming stars into certain groups and patterns called constellations? Were these to be story stars, used for signs as well as seasons, in some way spelling out His mysterious plan for this unique planet? Whatever this starry story would turn out to be, they knew Satan for sure had plans to twist it into something else entirely.

Back on the second and third days, in the evenings and mornings, the angels had thrilled to glimpse the sky, sea and land as they suddenly appeared. No wonder the Godhead had kept proclaiming "GOOD!" when such marvels as trees full of fruits and plants loaded with vegetables appeared. Not only was their immense variety amazing, but all the colors were stunning!

Actually, what the angels really delighted in the most were the Lord's signature love letters...the exquisite, dazzling diversity of perfumed FLOWERS! Recognizing some of their favorite scents, they guessed He had copied a few from heaven! Day five, however, was producing the biggest surprise so far: WHALES! Sea monsters, fantastic fish swarming all over the sea, and incredible birds flying all through the air! It was way beyond their wildest imaginations!

As the sixth day, the climax of Creation, was dawning, an electric excitement escalated in both armies of angels. Getting to see up close the Almighty team in action had been astounding! All of it was a cooperative project. The Father was the Mastermind; the Son, as His Word, did the work, and the Holy Spirit provided the dynamic energy.

Instantly, new life appeared! From huge and monstrous to tiny and microscopic, the Earth now teemed with animal forms of dizzying diversity! Watching them run, crawl, jump, climb, leap, scamper and gallop, the angels laughed and danced with joy at all the funny, cute and stupendous creatures. What a humorous imagination their Creator had! Was that why they chuckled a lot to themselves during the planning stages?

But what puzzled the angels was God blessing all these animals, birds and fish and then commanding them to MULTIPLY! What did that mean? How could they ever do that? Although there were many millions of angels, they had a fixed number. Each one had been directly made by the Most High. But they heard the Godhead announce "Let us make humans in Our image, according to Our likeness; and let them rule over...the Earth."[13]

Was this then to be the ultimate goal and purpose for this amazing planet? Would the Designer Of Intelligence make intelligent beings who could design and create things also? But what if these intelligent beings denied they were designed and claimed they just "happened" to "evolve" more or less by themselves? In that case, the angels decided they would probably self-destruct by their own intelligently designed devices.

Now they carefully moved in closer for an angel's eye view of God personally forming the one to be called "man" out of the ground of the Earth itself. Then, hearing something like wind, they were startled to see God Himself breathing what He called the "breath of life" into Adam (which was the name He gave the first human).

Having declared all of His Creation to be "very good," God did not want them to know and experience the evil that Satan had injected into heaven. So only one law would be given; to not eat of the tree of the knowledge of good and evil, which would result in spiritual death and gradual physical death. On the other hand, eating from the tree of life would keep him alive forever. And because He had created all the animals tame and vegetarian, they would not be dying either.[14]

Now the angels saw thousands of the fanciful creatures of Paradise being brought to Adam to get names. Some, although many times larger than the man, were quite docile and friendly. Climbing up their enormous tails, he could take a ride way up high on their spiky backs. Of course, some of the angels could ride with him, unaware and unseen. Being invisible did have its advantages even though God would allow them to be seen in the future.

As each animal paraded by, Adam spoke a name for it. God agreed to each name. Remembering them all would be no problem, because, of course, they both spoke the same language. Having created the first human in His own image, He also gave him a built-in communication system to talk to His Heavenly Father. However, seeing that it was not good for him to be alone and, since He had created mates for all the animals, it was time to create a helper-companion for Adam.

Putting him into a deep sleep, God painlessly removed a rib from his side, skillfully fashioning it into a beautiful human counterpart called woman. Without her he had not been complete. "In the image of God, male and female He created them." But now what? Would she just tend the Garden alongside him, or was there to be a unique dimension to their relationship unknown to angels?

All at once, the angels saw a strange, most peculiar thing happening. The animals had begun to connect their bodies together, two by two, in odd ways. What could this mean? Eventually, after observing half the creatures swelling up and little ones emerging from their bodies, (or from something called "eggs"), they began to understand. Might this be how God's edict of "multiply and fill the Earth" would be accomplished? What an incredible idea! Who else could have thought it up?

Meanwhile, Satan had been constantly stalking the two humans called man and woman. Finally catching sight of them under a palm tree, he watched them feeding each other dates. Moving in for a closer look, he wondered what power seemed to be drawing their bodies together like magnets! Not only did they have solid bodies called flesh and blood, but they had certain novel body parts the angels lacked. He saw a projectile in the middle of the man being inserted into an opening in the middle of the woman. Then, face to face, with their mouths clinging together, they made movements and emitted sounds of some sort of intense pleasure.

Obviously, they had discovered a means of great enjoyment! Rolling and laughing in the lush grass, they sang to the bluebirds and parrots darting high up in the palm trees. In their ecstasy, the two of them had become like one! Then, after much time had passed, the woman swelled up with a large protrusion on her front below two smaller pointed spheres. All of a sudden, with little effort, a small replica of her or her husband came out of that same opening. After that, by holding its mouth up to the pointed spheres, she caused it to drink some sort of food. When it grew larger it walked and talked just like a man and woman! So this was the mysterious union called "family" that the Most High had denied to the angels, who were unable to increase themselves. Burning with jealousy, Satan inflated his hatred to a new level![15]

PLAYGROUND OF THE GODS 6

⎯⎯☽❧⎯⎯

Although the crystal canopy of waters above the sky gave the daytime sun a soft, pink glow, it was the evenings in Eden that were most lovely. As the cool breeze caressed their skin, Adam and Eve walked and talked with God in the garden. Since they had cooperated with His request to "be fruitful and multiply," all of them laughed together at the play of their little ones, along with the curious baby animals. But even knowing the turmoil of the future, nothing could stop God from the immense enjoyment of these moments with His new family!

So did watching all this bliss from the sidelines cause a twinge of melancholy in Lucifer? Not exactly. Having left and lost the love of his Creator, Satan was getting furious at all these "family" forms of love. Something would have to be done about it or they would soon outnumber his kingdom forces. "Why hadn't angels been given these body parts with power to reproduce" he fumed? If they had, they could have multiplied all over the galaxies of the whole universe! With such vast numbers then, he calculated, they would have been able to overthrow the actual throne of the Most High! At last, they would rule their own way, without having to serve or obey any Creator God's laws!

Intoxicated by this ambition, the Devil's whole being swelled with a great surge of angel-potential. Could it possibly happen? Was there a way the impossible could be done? What if his angels could somehow leave their spirit forms and morph into humanoid bodies? By tampering with the genetic code, they might create an alternate race to kill off the people of God.

Meanwhile in the lush garden of Eden it was always spring and summertime and the living was easy. Insects never bothered anyone or anything. And in this atmosphere, a heavenly harmony hung like a cloud of glory all around the first family of the children of Earth.

But how could they know that the peace of heaven itself had already been shattered by angel wars...and that the spoils of this ongoing battle were to be their very own precious souls? On their evening strolls God had been gradually enlightening Adam and Eve about the realities of things in His universe. Since both of them had been directly created by His own hand, their brain power was awesome.

Photographic memory made it easy for them to call all the thousands of creatures and plants by their specific names.

But what really mattered was having total recall of every word God had said to them. However, their fatal flaw, the one thing they lacked, was fear of the consequences of breaking God's law. Exactly what Lucifer was betting on when he slipped his spirit body into a friendly dragon. Then, targeting the woman, he casually asked, "Did God really say you must not eat from any tree in the garden?" Eve explained that they could eat fruit from all the trees except the one in the middle of the garden, which would result in the death penalty.

Moving in for the kill, Satan boldly tested his denial strategy...the LIE...by hissing, "You will not surely die... for God knows that when you eat of it your eyes will be opened, and you will be like God, knowing good and evil."[16]

Why should he be foolish enough to tell her that it was only he, Lucifer, who had made God experience evil.... when betraying Him, and igniting the first war in the universe? Already, his challenge had gotten Eve thinking in a new mode. Instead of negative ideas of punishment, a positive mindset thrilled her imagination with human potential. Wasn't that forbidden fruit beautiful? Wasn't it going to be delicious and nutritious? And best of all, wasn't it going to give her great wisdom?

As spectator to this intrigue, her husband seemed to focus on the power of positive, possibility thinking: Why not just ignore that fearful, negative threat his loving Heavenly

Father had made? Didn't perfect love cast out fear? So when his beguiled wife plucked the fabulous fruit and sank her teeth into its luscious juiciness, Adam was happy to join in.

Instantly, this risky new adventure brought their whole world crashing down! Horrified, they suddenly felt naked. Although never having worn clothing, now the Holy Glory of God's covering was stripped away. Trembling, they fearfully emerged from their hiding place only at their Maker's call. As it turned out, He was not impressed with the fig leaf fashions they had sewn as a cover-up. Then the blame game began! Now the DNA of human nature had become infected with a sin gene which would plague all their future descendants.

Eve blamed the serpent-dragon for deceiving her. Adam blamed both his wife and God, even though he had not been deceived. So God, true to His word, pronounced a curse (with a cryptic promise) for all three of them. Ignoring the ominous promise of a future woman-seed to crush his head, Satan celebrated Operation-Eden as a great success. How could these miserable Earthlings ever defeat his kingdom?

Adam and Eve, the unique, handcrafted humans, were spinning in a whirlwind of new emotions. Dread, regret, and confusion were closing in with the burdens of multiple-choice to navigate their own way. Still, Godlike power to know good and evil would be exciting! But who knew what evil really was? Hadn't the serpent told them they needed it to be like God and get wisdom? But now, as they listened in shock to their first evil experience assignments, they weren't so sure it was going to be worth it.

For starters, the woman would have greatly increased pain in childbirth. And, even though she would still want sex with her husband, they wouldn't be cozy companions anymore, because he was now going to rule over her! This was going to get rough, since she was condemned to an all day, every day, struggle. For the man, it was going to be sweaty slaving over hard ground, trying to grow enough food among newly emerging thorns and thistles.[17] At this point, he might have been thinking, "Since I wasn't deceived, why didn't I strongly warn Eve it was a trap? Why didn't I rebuke that serpent and order him out of the garden? After all, didn't God give me dominion and authority over all His nature and creatures?"

But now he couldn't reverse that hypnotic apathy and he had to confess to a tantalizing curiosity himself. Being double-minded and slow to respond had been his downfall and, hating to admit it even to himself, he may not have wanted to risk antagonizing his source of sexual pleasures. Feeling depressed, it was nevertheless time to start learning how to become a ruler the hard way. And when he found out the real identity of that serpent, the battle of the ages would begin!

Finally finding courage to look at their Heavenly Father's face again, the man and woman saw anger and compassion mingled as the laser beam of His hand painlessly cut the throat of one of His animals. As a thick, intensely red liquid poured out, Adam and Eve were stunned! Having never seen blood or death, they were jolted with its power as the earthly life-force. But why wasn't it done to them? They bore the guilt of the crime, not the animal. Was this to be the pattern of sacrifice? To offer an innocent substitute? Would forgiveness come now?

Overwhelmed with sad and grateful feelings, tears flooded their faces and they were heartbroken over what they had done. But God, in His mercy, covered them with clothing made from the animal's skin. Suddenly they felt born from above, relieved and cleansed from all their shame!

Transfixed by this touching tableau, Lucifer and his legions were infuriated to see the humans given the second chance that they had been denied. Never again could they go home, but only roam the Earth and fly in its atmosphere until the end of the age (which they trembled to think about). But why dwell on the negative? Forget the mutating serpent species, now cursed to lose its legs because of his choice of disguise. Let them slither in the dust as snakes; he would elevate them to emblems of learning and liberty! Besides, he, Satan, could always morph into his ultimate image of a flying red dragon!

Enough of this contemplation. There was Kingdom work to be done! Actually, celebration was in order. Time for takeover was near. The celestial visitors were poised to appear. Contact would be made...such as the terrestrials had never dreamed. The "lords of the shining face" would arrive to start a new race. Now, Earth would become the playground of the gods and humans would be their toys!

7
THE WORLD
THAT DROWNED

—☙ ❧—

Outwardly, the dazzling splendor of Eden looked unchanged, but secretly, the DNA of all its creatures was being reprogrammed for slow decay and death. Strangely, now God had something to fear from man. How could He allow him to get immortality in his fallen condition?

"And the Lord God (Yahweh Elohim) said the man has now become like one of us, knowing good and evil. He must not be allowed to reach out his hand and take also from the tree of life and eat, and live forever."

Looking back, the first family wondered what would happen to the paradise of their gorgeous garden. Would exile from Eden last forever? In the distance, they spotted holy angels descending with what looked like fire-sabers. Blocking the east side of the garden, to guard the tree of life, a huge flaming sword appeared, flashing lightning sparks while spinning in all directions![18]

Now cosmic anarchy was about to come down to Earth. By the time the first murder was committed, with Cain killing his brother Abel, it was certain that humankind were carriers of a sin-virus that would someday break out into an epidemic called "War." Satan was wildly applauding this murder. It was the beginning of his job description! But why weren't the holy angels, who were appalled, allowed to stop this? Why would a good God allow humans to multiply atrocities on the Earth...causing innocent bystanders to suffer also? Why allow people to increase evil to the max before taking over by force to end it? Tragically, that time would have to come–sooner than anyone thought.

A celestial conspiracy was waiting for the signal to make their first appearance; to oblige the Earthlings' desire for more knowledge.

Here is the story of what actually happened, as told to an ancient historian and scribe by the Holy Spirit. Recording it as the true history of the world, it was preserved by the prophets God chose to write His Book.

"...when men began to multiply on the...
Earth, and daughters were born to them...
the supernatural beings (sons of God...fallen
angels) saw...that they were beautiful; and
they took wives for themselves of all whom
they chose...There were giants (Nephilim)
on the earth in those days, and also afterward,
when the sons of God came in to the daughters of men and they bore children to them.
Those were the mighty men (heroes)...of
old, men of renown" (famous legendary gods
of mythology)[19]

What was to be the result, the influence of this strange
new breed of demigods, and this unnatural race of giant
supermen on the Earth? Having been angels originally connected with the supernatural, these rebel princes became
instructors of humans in all sorts of occult (hidden) knowledge: Astrology, ritual magic, sorcery, alchemy and even the
genetic manipulation for creating animal-human hybrids–
many of which can still be seen depicted on the great mon-
uments of antiquity. Although these first "extra-terrestrials"
had brought information and skills for creating advanced
civilizations, there was a hidden agenda behind their friendly
first contact.

But who on Earth could resist these mystery teachers
of the heavens? The gigantic size of their superhuman

offspring, often twice as big as mere mortals, made it certain they would set themselves up as kings for both worship and war! What with strange circular lights and fires flashing around the skies, Earth people couldn't tell exactly what was real and unreal about some of these "space visitors."

However it wasn't long before the humans, snared by the beautiful side of evil, grew obsessed with sex and violence to the point of no return. Hearing the weird stories of the exploits and escapades of these gods, and feeling their hypnotic power, people began to be captivated and entranced. Reality and fantasy started to merge. Morality was a dim memory. Orgies of perversion spread worldwide. Eating, drinking, and mating involved all ages, genders, and species, ending in addictions to drugs and blood. All creation was sinking into a culture of death, and Satan, who had obtained the power of death, couldn't have been more thrilled!

> "And God saw that the wickedness of man was great in the Earth, and that every imagination of the thoughts of his heart was only evil continually.

> "And the Lord was sorry that he had made man on the Earth, and He was grieved in His heart."

What possible solution was left? All this time God's Spirit had been striving with humans. But now, suffering total rejection, He had no choice but to wipe them all out and start over again! Finally, God said to Noah, the only faithful person He could find on Earth;

"I will destroy...both man and beast...for I am sorry I have made them...for the Earth is filled with violence through them...and behold, I myself am bringing the flood of water on Earth, to destroy from under heaven all flesh in which is the breath of life; and everything that is on the Earth shall die"[20]

But somehow, Noah's extended family, plus samples of the animal and food creation, would have to be preserved as survivors to begin a new population. Telling Noah to construct a great, extravagant box boat, the Lord had a plan to preserve the only godly family through the flood. How else could His promise of the future "Seed of the woman" avoid failure? After all, the whole destiny of the planet depended on it.

Being 450 feet long, 75 feet wide, and 45 feet high, the "Ark" was necessarily huge! With thousands of cages built on three enclosed deck levels, the Creator had designed it so that no species would be left behind, even the young dinosaurs. But, though more than 100 years would be allowed for construction, how could anyone ever believe a flood would come? Nobody had yet seen rain! Earth still received only the morning mist that went up to water the ground. So what exactly was a flood and where would it come from anyway? No one knew. And besides, their "helper-angels" had told them God would never send the gloom and doom of destruction anyway. It was all just a myth...to spoil their obscene fun!

Since the demonizing of planet Earth was well underway, ridicule and mockery of Noah and his three sons was especially shrill and profane. After long exhausting days of chopping trees and dragging logs, their wives comforted them with dreams of escape. Able to help with some of the building jobs too, they wanted a break from growing, gathering and storing all the huge amounts of every kind of food. Often, they hoped and prayed that at least a few people would come to their senses, return to God, and join them in the Ark.[21]

But despite worldwide publicity warning about the reason for "Noah's insane project," the downward spiral of depravity and corruption continued. The Lord was heartbroken, but had to go ahead with His drastic plan. By accessing radar-like instincts, their creator was able to direct all the male and female pairs of animals into the Ark. His holy angels were also helping to coordinate from the spirit realm, guarding against the hindering and harassment of intruding demons.

Even after the family of eight worthy persons was safely inside the Ark, God still waited a whole week longer to see if anybody else would take Him seriously. No one did. So He sadly shut the door Himself. Now the long predicted deluge would finally be unleashed. What people never seemed to realize was that, once God had spoken something, it HAD to happen. He could not lie. At His Word, the crystal canopy of waters in the sky came crashing down, dumping billions of gallons on Earth. People screamed and mobbed the Ark, pounding desperately on its sealed door. Those who were able climbed to the roof, just to gasp for air a few hopeless minutes longer.

Then massive undersea volcanoes erupted, sending incredible walls of "tsunami" tidal waves. "Enlightened" civilizations, such as the fabled Atlantis, suddenly sank out of sight. Both humans and animals were clawing their way to the top of mountains, only to be struck by earthquakes that split open to swallow them alive. Every form of life on Earth was sinking under the rapidly rising floodtide.[22]

Immense strata layers were formed by intense pressure, as vegetation, sediment and creatures were sandwiched together, creating future fossils and oil deposits deep under the Earth. As the box-boat Ark floated and rolled up above on the waves, protecting its precious cargo, vast and awesome canyons were being sculpted underneath.

Fish and sea shells were tossed onto newly rising mountain tops. Enormous beasts were flash-frozen with bunches

61

of flowers still in their mouths as the poles of the planet shifted. Weren't all these oddities to boggle the minds of scientists many centuries later? Denying any such "folklore" as a global flood with Noah's Ark, they would say it all just happened by itself over billions of years. That way, nobody could ever have seen it to make an eyewitness report–least of all "God"!

It was as if the world had drowned in the tears of its loving Creator, from sorrow over His masterpiece called Earth being defiled and ruined by its occupants.

8
TOWER POWER

tuck on the rocky top of the newly elevated mountains on Ararat, the Ark rested until the waters receded. But Noah had mixed emotions about leaving it. He knew that when he set foot on dry ground again it would be covered with millions of mangled, decayed bodies. Pieces of people and animals would be scattered everywhere as a grim reminder of the cost of total rebellion.

Still, he wondered, how many new generations would pass before they might forget the flood, or deny the reasons for it? Worst of all, they might censor the real story and reinvent it as just a fairy tale for children! A deep sigh shook his spirit, but these dark thoughts fled as Noah lifted up his arms in praise to the Most High. Why shouldn't he be thankful for being chosen as the new father of all future humankind?

What an awesome privilege and responsibility for his tiny family. After more than a year, he couldn't even imagine the changes that awaited them outside the Ark. Little did he know that two new seasons would begin in many parts of the planet. Fall and winter were to be strange new experiences.

Suddenly everyone was cheering! The dove Noah had sent out just returned with an olive leaf in her beak. Somebody suggested it might become an international peace symbol someday. What crazy imaginations, thought Noah, his sons had after being so long on the Ark! Slowly, all this shouting was waking up the animals out of their divinely imposed hibernation. And, at long last, it was time to open the door and look at what was left of the world.

As they heard God's voice telling them to leave, everyone crowded out of the Ark–an amazing entourage, parading past their Maker by species (which He called "families"). But, first things first! Quickly building an altar of stones, Noah sacrificed some of His creatures back to their Creator in thanksgiving. As he enjoyed the pleasing aroma, the Almighty surprised them with a unique, new thing in the sky!

Looking up, the little flood family was amazed to see a vast, striped arch of seven glowing colors. Spanning the sky like an immense bridge from east to west, it was to be called a rainbow! Then the Most High announced its purpose:

> "I have set my rainbow in the clouds, and it
> will be the sign of the covenant between Me

and the Earth...never again will the waters become a flood to destroy all life. Whenever the rainbow appears in the clouds, I will see it and remember the everlasting covenant between God and all living creatures of every kind on the Earth."[23]

But as exciting as all this was, the eight survivors couldn't help feeling shocked at the new laws the Lord had also given them. The new reality was that the animals would now fear them, since they were told to start eating meat as well as plants. But blood was absolutely forbidden, because it contained the life of the creature. Only after they drained it all out onto the ground could the meat be cooked and eaten.

For the first time, humans would have to learn how to become hunters and gatherers, just as they had begun farming when exiled from the easy fruit picking of Eden. But what Noah couldn't figure out was how the animals, especially the dinosaurs, would survive on just the leftovers of flood-ravaged vegetation.

Then, realizing the truth, he had to face the fact that all nature was now out of order. Many animals would begin mutating into carnivores. Of necessity, much of the creation had to become "red in tooth and claw." Noah prayed that never again would such an extreme level of sin sweep the Earth like an epidemic. A chill shivered his spine at the thought, but after hearing God's new law, he wasn't so sure!

For the first time, the Most High was requiring the death penalty for anyone, even an animal, who killed a human: because as He said, they were created in the image of God. Hearing this, Noah felt shocked and bewildered. How could this be accomplished? Gathering his family, they all prayed that the fear of the Lord would stop murderers so they wouldn't have to carry out executions. Just the thought of having to track down and kill killers made them all shudder! But, how else could God stop the uncontrollable crime rate before the flood from exploding again?[24]

As the survivors of the whole creation slowly made their way down the mountains into a totally unpopulated Earth, the spirits of another realm were brainstorming again! Wasn't the recent great death harvest of detested mortals their surpassing victory? Jubilant celebration broke out among Lucifer's legions, with crescendos of curses reaching a fever pitch. Satan's eyes glowed blood red with excitement as he organized his next think tank. Wouldn't his top geniuses come up with a unique solution to squelch this new death penalty as a so-called sin deterrent? But who could have guessed the long-term unstoppable onslaught of the plan they pronounced? Once begun, it would increase automatically...forever! How about calling it WAR–an extension on Earth of what they had long ago invented in heaven!

Now who might be found to launch this new world order? Though years later, while many were willing to forget the flood, Lucifer was on the lookout for a very special person...a rebel after his own heart! Satan needed to set up his first proxy king on the Earth, so he himself could be the real power behind the throne!

But wasn't God's aversion to human kings well known? He had always wanted to rule in human hearts by invitation only, of course. Even so, His Holy Spirit was always busy drawing the minority out to form His forever family.

Meanwhile, scanning the landscape, the devil discovered Babylon. What a perfect place for his throne, right near the spot at the great river Euphrates where God had bound four of his top killer angels, the Titans. Though unseen and immobilized, maybe they might still be able to exert some spirit power. Anyway, this would be it...the future fountainhead of astrology, wizardry, sorcery, and idolatry. Babylon the great!

Satan's attention was riveted. Who was this fierce-faced giant in a leopard skin followed by troops of reveling women? It was the son of Cush (Bar Cush/aka Bacchus), a great grandson of Noah. Whispered thoughts came into Nimrod's mind, and his own spirit began to agree with what the invisible spirit was speaking. "Aren't you one of a new breed of giants, more god than human, because your mother was seduced by a Nephilim? Aren't you the most powerful and mighty hunter, chosen to avenge yourself on the Lord for destroying your giant forefathers in the flood?

"If you will build fortified cities, I will see to it that you are deified as the god of fortresses. By training a large army of young men for the mass murder of war, you will make a mockery of God's new death penalty law. Go forth conquering to enslave your unprepared neighbors. Expand and unify your empire with a tower of power for my star worship temple on top. Go and avenge your drowned ancestors and break the bands of the Almighty off the people and I will give you my power and my throne! You will be my Messiah King of Babylon!"

After opening himself to this enlightening spirit, Nimrod felt a surge of supernatural energy and wasted no time beginning his building boom...Babylon, Nineveh and five other cities in ancient Iraq (Uruk). Hadn't he long since established a reputation for himself as the mighty hunter-rebel in the face of the Lord? But now, many would speak his name with awe...as Lucifer's chosen agent on the Earth, even with the future possibility of receiving his power and his throne.[25]

But doesn't every king need a queen? Doesn't a god need a goddess? All Nimrod's allies, who wanted to make a name for themselves had been busy building the ziggurat Tower of Babel out of sun-baked bricks.[26] Then it happened. Seeing the throne room emerging, along came stunning Semiramis with long golden hair. Captivated by this goddess daughter of the sun, Nimrod had met his match (and, as it turned out...a whole lot more!).

Under cover of so-called nature fertility rites, they would create the first mystery religion of sex, violence and human sacrifice, even cannibalism, (as high priest of Baal – "Cahna-Bal"). But as Moloch (king), his specialty would be demanding the offering of children to his idol by fire. Secret rituals of initiation would bind the people in fear by oaths and curses. Demons devised elaborate charades of protection, blessing and calamity to convince everyone of their idol's power.

But was Semiramis satisfied with just being Queen of Babylon and mother of prostitutes and abominations? Or did she dream of a plan to eclipse Nimrod, steal his worship and become Queen of Heaven? By now, the majority were getting tired of holy living by the covenant of Noah. Yearning for the psychic power they heard about happening before the flood, once again they were rejecting the true love of their Creator. Still, He patiently waited, knowing He would have to let things get a lot worse on His testing ground planet, before they could get better.

69

WHITE HORSE FORCE:
Book One

Who Can Make Me a *Super-Immortal?*

PART THREE

KEEPERS OF THE ANCIENT ORACLES
The Story of Your Helpers

9
A SON NAMED LAUGHTER

⸺◌◌⸺

Like bees swarming around a hive, thousands of sweaty laborers climbed the great Tower of Babel with their burdens of bricks. As they built, rising higher toward the sun each day, excitement mounted while reminding each other it would soon reach to the heavens! Then, all of a sudden, right in mid-sentence, the words in their mouths actually changed! Many new languages started coming out and hardly any of them could understand one another. Shocked, confused and terrified, they wondered what could possibly have happened. Who had the power to put new varieties of words on their tongues instantly? Certainly nobody on Earth.

More crawling than climbing, they slowly moved down the sacred pyramid-mountain in bewildered silence, just leaving the bricks where they lay. After reaching the base, a frenzy of searching, sign language and re-grouping took place. Finally, collecting their families and camping with those who could understand each other, they tried to figure out what was next.

Dejection was everywhere. Who had interrupted their great dream...and why? Not seeing into the spirit realm, however, there was no way to have known the drama that had just happened in another dimension.

> "The Lord came down to see the city and the tower which the sons of men had built...they are one people, and they all have the same language...and now nothing which they plan to do will be impossible for them. Come, let US go down there and confuse their language so they will not understand each other...So the Lord scattered them abroad from there over the face of the whole Earth..."[27]

Not even Nimrod knew what to do. To an outsider, it must have looked rather strange–but that was the problem; there were no outsiders! Only by a communication gap could they be created.

Who knew that God's goal was a diversity of cultures living in nations all over the Earth? He didn't want a billion clones of Adam and Eve! But this time, He was taking no chances of the lightning-fast spread of evil due to a single language like before the flood. Atlantis would not rise again anytime soon, despite the nostalgia Lucifer always conjured up for it.

Did the arrogant tower-builders think that the Most High hadn't overhead them wanting to just stay put? Since they were refusing to spread out around the world, there was no choice but to go down and garble their speech. After all, who better than the Godhead knew that words were packages of power? Wasn't that exactly what they had used to create everything in the whole universe?

Meanwhile, the King and Queen of Babylon weren't happy about what was happening to their empire. People continued to disappear; moving out for parts unknown, all speaking languages unknown! As for the crowd left behind, God gave up on them to continue their towering obsession with Nimrod. And though forcibly put on hold for a while, it would eventually be built as the fountainhead of all false religions and exported to every corner of the globe!

Inevitably, at the apex of his tyrannical power, some of Nimrod's many enemies finally succeeded in killing him. This was carried out in the most extreme manner of those times, which included cutting his body up in pieces. His followers were frantic! After proclaiming him to now be a god, they went into a frenzy of weeping, wailing and cutting their bodies in his honor. Naturally, Semiramis was taking note of this bloodletting orgy orchestrated by the demons in her husband's behalf, and she wanted in on it.

This was the time she had been waiting for–to start a story so fantastic that, if believed, would make her famous (and infamous) forever! Getting herself pregnant by nobody knows who, she claimed that her new baby was actually her dead husband, Nimrod, REINCARNATED! Naming him "Ninus," she promoted him to be worshipped as a deity while being held in her arms. This new cult took off like a comet, and soon it was clear that she, as the Goddess Mother, was the real power to be sought after and adored. It didn't take long for her new title, "Queen of Heaven" to confer great celebrity and star status way beyond Babylon.

Another innovation would turn out to be immensely popular. Although the Three-Person form of the Godhead had been known since earliest times (from Eden), Semiramis now made an adjustment and inserted herself in place of the Holy Spirit. As a result, the demons that possessed her have continually impersonated various Mother and Child goddesses worldwide in dazzling apparitions. What they teach, in their sweet loving way however, is always the same lie; that ALL religions are just different, acceptable paths to God, and that the "Queen of Heaven" is the mediator to pray to.

After great success in Babylon, the new legend was ready to go global as the first multicultural mystery religion. Eventually, mourners would be screaming and gashing themselves at the same time of the year in nations on every continent, weeping for the violent death of the mystical Nimrod, by whatever name he was known locally. After that, it was an awesome thrill to bow to the idol of his goddess wife, holding him reborn as her baby son (both of whom had also undergone ethnic name changes, worldwide).

Finally, Satan was satisfied that this system had it all with the long range potential to imitate, counterfeit, confuse and infiltrate anything God might put out! Thanks to Nimrod and Semiramis, Lucifer's link between power, money, sex and religion was irresistibly forged.

Once again, the Mastermind of the universe was feeling like a wounded lover. Would God be able to find another faith-friend on the Earth? Then while reading the mind of a man named Abram, He liked what he saw. The wealthy semi-nomad tribesman was beginning to feel like an alien on Earth. Having heard the warnings of Noah's son Shem, who was still alive, he knew that the images of the local pop culture depicted demons. They were the imposter "gods" who, as angels, had rebelled against the real God, their Creator.

Abram was dreaming that somehow he could find a celestial city built by God Himself, with eternal heavenly foundations somewhere out in space...not mystical, but incredibly real![28] He and his wife moved with the rest of his family from southern Babylonia (Chaldea) north to Aram (Syria). During their sojourn at a great caravan trading center, the God of Glory appeared and told him to leave his family for an unknown land. Not sure why His Creator would call him out[29] Abram knew only that the VOICE had pierced through his very bones and into his heart like a two-edged sword of fire, and he would never be the same again!

In fact, the Most High had His eye on a certain enemy land. Settled by people under a curse, Canaan was named for the son of Ham who had dishonored his grandfather, Noah.[30] What awesome, eternal plans did God secretly have for this unique land? Why did He promise to give it to Abram's descendants when he and his wife, Sarai were childless? What they didn't know was that God considered her, at 60, too young for what He had in mind! What would be a more hilarious miracle than a 90 year old woman walking around pregnant with her first baby? And when He told them about it, of course they laughed! So He said to name the boy Laughter! (Yitzhak, aka Isaac).[31] (And how many comedians came from this child's descendants in the 20th century alone?) Then God changed their names: Abram would be "Abraham" (father of multitudes of nations), and Sarai would become "Sarah" (princess).

Now what was that great outcry rising to the throne of the Most High? It vibrated through all dimensions! Like a cancer on Canaan, a massive concentration of sex atrocity was attacking planet Earth. The year was 1898 B.C. and several cities in the lush Jordan valley, where Abraham's nephew, Lot, had settled, were now targeted for destruction. But how would Lot's family be able to escape in time? And what would happen to all his riches and flocks and herds?

Showing up as three men at Abraham's tent, the Lord and two warrior angels came down to investigate. After enjoying the hospitality of food and drink always given to travelers, the angels headed down to check out the report, while the Lord decided to reveal the plan to His friend.

Finally, after Abraham negotiated all the way down from 50, the Lord agreed not to destroy the city if only 10 decent men could be found in it.[32] But it was not to be. Like a wall to wall wolf pack, the great mob of men, young and old, rushed toward Lot's house. Assuming them to be mere men, they stalked the two new visitors in town, desperate for gang rape.

Unaware they were sent from space on a search and destroy mission, the Sodomites violently slammed against Lot's door, demanding that he bring the men out. Instantly, the angels blinded them all and urged the family to evacuate quickly so they could activate the incineration. Though they were all warned not to look back when it happened Lot's wife did because she probably hated to leave her affluent lifestyle.

> "Then the Lord rained down burning sulfur on Sodom and Gomorrah...out of the heavens. Thus He overthrew...the entire plain, in the land. But Lot's wife looked back, and she became a pillar of salt."[33]

THE TEMPESTUOUS AFFAIR 10

⸺ʚ ɞ⸺

From his vantage point above the valley, Abraham watched the black smoke of Sodom rising as a vast funeral pyre. Like a reservoir of salty tears for these perished souls, would the Dead Sea now overflow it forever? Still, Abraham recalled, this area was to be part of his promised future land. Wouldn't the Lord someday restore and heal it? Had not God made many covenants with him as he walked through Canaan? Once, at night, after sacrificing the required animals, a terrible foreboding had come over him as the Almighty spoke about his descendants becoming slaves in a foreign land for 400 years. Feeling bewildered, Abraham wondered why the offspring of his miracle son named Laughter would have to suffer so much before getting a country of their own.

However, in another dimension unseen by him, hostile entities had been watching this same scene. While he had been absorbed in thought, Satan had issued a summons for a summit with his hierarchy of darkness. Scowling and prowling like an unfed lion, he ranted and raged in disbelief at how the greatest stronghold of his kingdom had totally gone up in smoke! How could his angels have allowed those Sodomites to even attempt attacking enemy angels? What could his princes have been thinking? Now it would be back to square one; training and indoctrinating these mortals from youth on that sex is nothing but a recreational sport with anyone or anything.

When God surveyed the smoldering ruins, He wasn't happy about it either. But seeing His angels playing with and singing to the little children who escaped from Sodom to heaven, He was comforted. At last, they were set free from the pornographic nightmare of their wounded lives of suffering sexual abuse. The babies being burned in the fire of the idol god, Moloch, were escaping that horror also. Therefore, even though nobody knew it, not even His friend Abraham, God couldn't wait to activate His long range plan to get Earth back to Eden conditions. He had to do it…for the children!

Life was good in Canaan. Really good. The land was full of figs and grapes, milk, honey and olives. Every sort of fruit was on the trees and there was no limit to any kind of cattle. Bread and wine, cooked meat and roast fowl were plentiful. Being semi-nomads, Abraham's camp settled near larger towns, while avoiding the cities of the giants.

But why had these Nephilim made a comeback after the flood? Hadn't the first wicked angels who produced them been locked up in the abyss in Tartarus, the lowest level of the underworld? Now what if these new invaders multiplied to make a murderous future challenge to God's people?

As a base of operations, and fields to plant his grain every spring, Abraham had bought land for a family burial ground. Pitching his tent in the area of Hebron, it was the only spot he owned in the whole land God had promised to give him; but when, he wondered.[34] His son, Isaac, having been brought up by a mother who looked like a great grandmother, was 40 years old by the time she died. Knowing he could no longer put off finding a wife for Isaac, Abraham decided his trusted steward should be the one to search.

Saddling ten camels with gifts and gold jewelry, he was sent up to Syria on a quest to find the right bride among relatives still there. Isaac was in romantic suspense to see who she might be. As the supernatural son and heir, it had long been explained to him why the local Canaanite girls were unacceptable. For one thing, they could be called upon to do sacred prostitute service in their community idol temples. And who knew how long their families would allow a Hebrew husband to opt out of bowing down to Baal, Ashtaroth and other obscene gods?

In that era, Abraham was one of the few who had fled from it all. Having grown up in Ur, the center of Chaldean mystic magic, he knew that the family God had told him to leave might still be into idolatry, but the girl chosen for Isaac would have to leave it behind!

Unaware that she was enacting a prearranged signal, Rebekah (Rivkah) told the stranger approaching her village well, "Drink, my lord...and...I'll draw water for your camels too." When the mystery traveler then put gold jewelry on her nose and arms, Rebekah realized with a thrill that her secret dreams were really coming true. Somehow, she had always wanted to seek a mysterious man in a strange land who would be her true love and soul mate forever, even though she had never yet seen him.

But she knew in her spirit it was the truth when this wealthy man's servant told her an angel had gone before him to reveal her as the chosen bride for his master's son. The next day, after lavish gifts had been presented, her family asked her: "Will you go with this man?" She said, "I will go." And as it turned out, she was the granddaughter of Abraham's brother (Isaac's uncle) and their household sent her off with this blessing: "Our sister, may you increase to thousands upon thousands; may your offspring possess the gates of their enemies."

As they came into Canaan on camels, Isaac looked up from his field in the Negev just as Rebekah saw him. Quickly she covered herself with a veil, and he took her into his mother's tent. She became his wife and he loved her.[35] Later on, finding she was unable to have children, Isaac prayed in desperation to the Lord on her behalf. At last, how overjoyed they were when it was discovered that she was actually pregnant with twins! Some months later, however, her elation was turning into turmoil. What could be happening? It felt like the two babies were battling insider her! Finally, going to God for an answer, the Lord said to Rebekah:

> "Two nations are in your womb, Two peoples shall be separated from your body; One people shall be stronger than the other, And the older shall serve the younger."[36]

Even while speaking those words, God knew it was to be a setup for sorrow. Would His experiment in nation-building really work? He knew, of course, that getting up close and personal with one people group would cost Him untold grief. For this infant family, being birthed from Laughter (Isaac), a disastrous and glorious roller coaster relationship lay ahead. In fact, the nation to come from one of these twins would have a love/hate tempestuous affair with the Most High for the next 4,000 years!

11
HOOKED BY A BOOK

C amped at night while traveling with all the family
and possessions he had acquired, Yakov (Jacob)
feared for his life. His wives and eleven sons and
one daughter lay sleeping in their tents, but his heart was
heavy. And why wouldn't he be terrified? Didn't a mes-
senger just tell him his twin brother, Esau, was coming with
400 warriors?[37]

Looking back on it all, he wondered about that fateful
prophecy the Lord had given his mother. Why had he come
out of her womb grabbing his brother's heel? Was it self-de-
fense to push it away from his face? Now his soul was
tormented by the outcome. But hadn't Esau despised his
inheritance and agreed to sell his birthright for a bowl of
lentil stew? Famished with hunger from his hunting trip, he
hadn't thought twice about it.[38]

Knowing God's promise to Him, should he, Jacob, have obeyed his mother's plan to get the deathbed blessing of his father when Isaac was too blind to know which son it was? After that, he had only averted Esau's vow to kill him by escaping north to his relatives in Haran (Syria). Had all the years of hard labor for his uncle, (who had tricked and cheated him many times) been worth it? Yes! Because he had his true love, Rachel, as well as her sister for wives, plus many sons and vast wealth of flocks and herds. The Lord had blessed him amazingly. But now, it was all at risk and his life was on the line.

As he was agonizing and praying over his past, some sort of a Man emerged from the shadows and wrestled with him. Exerting all his strength, Jacob felt compelled to cling to Him all night to demand a blessing. The odd thing was that he called this Man God, and received from Him both a name change and a limp! He said: "Your name shall no longer be Yakov, but Israel, because you have struggled with God and with men and have overcome."[39]

But why, he wondered, would the Son of God be making these mysterious appearances as a Man on the Earth? And why would He begin to add the names of three humans to His own name? What was to be the point of Him identifying himself from now on as "the God of Abraham, Isaac and Jacob" or "the God of Israel" or the "Holy One of Israel?" Eventually, it would take a Book to figure that out!

Unaware of that destiny, Jacob knew at dawn, a strategy had come to him for dealing with the threat of Esau. When the plan actually worked, they embraced in peace, for the time being. Now, Israel and his family would live, and twelve tempestuous tribes would spring from his sons. But during that fateful night, when he got a new name, he realized the Lord would be faithful to all His promises, even when they weren't. Would Israel deserve it? Of course not. No other nation of humans would either.[40]

Long, long ago, in the counsels of the Most High, it had been decreed that a Book would have to be written explaining God's ways to Earth dwellers. A certain people would have to be appointed for the job, and over many centuries their prophets would receive and record His words. Knowing that thousands of years later there would be youth on the Earth asking, "Is there a God and did He leave any messages?" He had to plan far ahead. For them especially, He would have to have the technology in place to instantly reach the greatest global population in history. This would be the last generation of His white horse force formation. Before heaven's scheduled takeover of Earth, the book of future forecasts, warning of this occupation army of immortals, is what motivated the Most High. How else could the Creator communicate the true history of the world?

Satan's subordinates would be busy from the beginning putting their spin on it...even seducing God's own people with brilliant but bogus "facts." Truly, it would be a Book to die for and many would have to, in order to preserve it intact. But before the final showdown, every language group would have access to at least a few of the most powerful pages.

However, how would humans know it was from Him and not just made up by men? Simple. A lot of the terrible sins and atrocities of His chosen nation would be recorded in it by themselves (something never done by other nations). Detailed future predictions would be included to test its supernatural accuracy...even hundreds and thousands of years later...(something never done in other "holy books"). Ultimately, what would be the purpose for this project? The answer: To expose the reasons for the human condition and world situation at any given time, and to provide the only workable solution. Real life stories of His people would furnish examples and insight. This unique Book was to be the mirror for the multitude and Israel would be its handle!

Around 1875 B.C., when extreme famine struck Canaan, all 70 of Israel's family headed down to Egypt.[41] Food was available there but at a price. They had friends in high places, so they soon flourished and prospered under the favor of the Pharaoh. Finally, when a less than friendly Pharaoh ruled, they were suddenly trapped. Hospitality had turned into slavery! How would their numbers, now being enormous, ever escape (as mere shepherds) from the all-powerful military might of the top ruling nation of the world? When the Egyptian king decreed all Hebrew boy babies must be killed, it looked like the end indeed for Israel.[42]

Moses, a prince of Egypt rescued as a baby and raised by the king's daughter, strangely found himself hiding out on the backside of the desert in Arabia herding sheep. Why had he lost all control and yielded to his urge to kill when he saw the torture of his Hebrew people? Now he was staring transfixed at a fire that didn't burn the bush it surrounded. As the voice of God came out of the fire saying he was to go back to lead his people out of Egypt, Moses gave God an argument. But, in the end, he had to obey when a promise was given for his brother Aaron to do the talking.[43]

Frogs filled Pharaoh's face. Their bug eyes eyed him. His whole palace, his whole country, was one huge frog bog. Yesterday, all the waters had turned to blood. After that, plagues of gnats and flies followed. As a mockery from the Most High, Egypt was being buried in its own gods. But even when disease wiped out their cattle, boils broke out on everyone, extreme hail and locusts destroyed most of their crops and total darkness fell for three days, still the Pharaoh hardened his heart and refused to let the Israelites leave![44]

His defiant attitude was that, even if God destroyed his whole nation, he still wouldn't let God's people go. Finally Moses gave him the Lord's last message: "Israel is My firstborn son, and I told you 'Let my son go, so that he may worship Me.' But you refused to let him go; so I will kill your firstborn son."

Each Israelite, seeing the red band of blood spurt on the little white lamb, as its neck was quickly cut for a painless sacrifice, knew the household children were saddened. Growing up among shepherds, it had been a familiar sight to them, but because this lamb had lived in the house four days, he seemed like a special pet. Nevertheless, God had ordered each family of Israel to do this for their own protection. Promising to pass over every house where He saw the blood of the lamb on the door frames, the Lord would not allow the death angel to enter and kill their firstborn sons.

But at midnight, it was a different story for all the Egyptians, including their king. In the dead of night, a great woeful wailing rose up all over the land. Every family in the whole country, from the lowest slaves to the Pharaoh's palace, had found their firstborn dead. But the Promise of Passover liberated the Lord's family. It had happened exactly as He told Moses to say. However, after Pharaoh finally relented and said Israel could get out of Egypt, he began having second thoughts.

For hundreds of years, Satan had been waiting for this moment! In fact, Lucifer was laughing all the way to the Red Sea. He had seen his demon gods devastated by the Almighty and his showcase culture in Egypt destroyed. Hadn't his whole kingdom cringed when the wonders God gave Moses and Aaron enabled them to overthrow the magic of Pharaoh's magicians? Who could have imagined, as all their rods turned into snakes that Aaron's snake would eat up all their demon snakes?

But nobody could rescue this Hebrew slave rabble now. They would never conquer their so-called promised land and break his stranglehold on Canaan! It would stay cursed and corrupt forever! The Son of God would never get His hands on its citadel city to enforce His law on this world! Hadn't Adam and Eve subleased it to him, Satan, the serpent-dragon, to be god of this cosmos? As prince of the power of the air, nothing could get by him. Or could it?

Lucifer felt this nothing nation from Abraham, Isaac, and Jacob would be finished off before they even got started. Still, he wondered why his arch-rival holy angels were the ones to recruit Pharaoh and his whole army to follow Israel to the Red Sea?

So what if there was that pesky pillar of cloud and fire leading them all the time? What could that do to save them from the greatest military superpower? Enough of all these humiliations of his hierarchy! He would avenge the deaths of his Egyptian servants by wiping out Israel's twelve tribes![45]

At the beginning of their exodus, while camped on the edge of the shore wedged between mountains and the Red Sea, the whole two million escapees were terrified. Pharaoh and his enormous Egyptian army had caught up and were waiting behind to recapture their slaves and kill as many as they wanted to. But Moses impossibly had said, "Stand still and see the salvation of the Lord." What could He do to get them out of this massacre waiting to happen?

Nobody had ever dreamed the supernatural spectacle which only the Most High Himself could manufacture to rescue His people against all odds. During the night, a roaring in the sky was heard. God had gotten busy sending his wind to make a bone dry road right through the middle of the sea, with no mud! Massive walls of water stood straight up on either side, and stayed that way until all of Israel had walked through with their children, herds of animals and the multi-cultural multitude who joined them.

Why hadn't Pharaoh and his troops followed? They couldn't until the Lord removed His pillar of dark cloud engulfing them. After that, the chariots rushed into the new sea road to pursue the people who were just reaching the opposite shore in Arabia. When the whole army got in, God collapsed the heaped up walls of His water wonder…and the rest is history. Erupting in song along with Moses, the whole multitude sent up praises to God in detailed story. "Then Miryan the prophetess, Aaron's sister, took a tambourine in her hand, and all the women followed her with tambourines and dancing. Miryan sang to them:

> "Sing to the Lord,
> For he is highly exalted.
> The horse and its rider
> He has hurled into the sea."[46]

For their little children, this was the most fantastic adventure of all, and they would be the only ones to live to tell about it! As for Moses, he was about to discover the reason for his princely education; to write the foundation of the Book to change the world! But would Israel succeed as the keepers of these ancient oracles to help everyone on the planet?

12
KILL THE MESSENGER NATION

_____ ᏍᎣ _____

O nly by continual miracles of water from rocks and food from the sky did the Lord finally get His nervous nation to His holy mountain (Horeb/Sinai) in Arabia. But why had He gone to so much trouble to get them all there? They were clueless about what to expect and wondered what the reason was for this rugged rendezvous? After sinking the soldiers of Egypt in the sea, why didn't the Lord's pillar of cloud and fire just fly them straight up to Canaan? Why this detour?

Rockets of flames shot up from the mountaintop and some smothered its steep slopes. God's descent on Horeb was horrendous to Israel, camped far down below. Somehow, despite the quaking, shaking and burning, Moses managed to reach the summit. While protected in the awesome presence of Yahweh, he was handed ten eternal laws written by the hand of the Most High Himself!

For one thing, to commemorate His creation, time would be split into sevens. Each week would have six days of work and a seventh day of rest; to remember Him and contemplate His blessings in thankfulness.

That decree alone set them apart from everyone else, but the major law would always get them into big trouble. By outlawing idols, He was putting them at odds with every other nation. This was extremely radical and the exact opposite of inclusive tolerance. How could they avoid being hated for insisting there is only One God? The code of ordinances that followed would really make them counter-culture from their neighbors. Because it even told them what to eat and what not to eat, they wouldn't be feasting with the other nations.

But that was the plan, the strategy of the Supreme Being. As a Father longs for His lost children to return, so the heart of the Most High wanted His national family to be a magnet for many to seek Him. This ten commandment core of the covenant was a blueprint for the Book that would follow. Suppose Israel didn't obey it? Would it still endure?

The year was 539 B.C. Belshazzar, King of Babylon (Iraq), was throwing a great wine feast for 1,000 of his nobles. In a one mile long banquet hall, 35,000 musicians played, while peacocks pulled little chariots piled with food around horse-shoe shaped tables. Night after night and day after day, the sumptuous parade of obscene opulence continued. And why not? Wasn't his kingdom the most fabled and vast empire of all? Wasn't he just following the tradition of its ancient founder, Nimrod? But then he made his big mistake...

> "...he gave orders to bring in the gold and silver goblets that Nebuchadnezzar (his ancestor) had taken from the temple in Jerusalem...and the king of his nobles, his wives and his concubines drank from them. As they drank the wine they praised the gods of gold and silver, of bronze, iron, wood and stone." (Daniel 5:2-4)

At the very zenith of this one mile marathon orgy, an unheard of horror happened. With his eyes riveted to a wall being written on by a disembodied Hand, the king sobered up fast! But why should only four words on a wall leave him in knee-knocking terror? Was it some kind of code? Belshazzar was bewildered and baffled. And why were all his sorcerers, wizards, magicians and astrologers clueless? None of them could decipher it, even after being offered royal robes and the third highest rulership of the kingdom.

Feeling the panic of doom closing in on him, the king's face turned pale. But when the queen heard all the commotion, she rushed in with the solution.

"Don't be alarmed! Don't look so pale! There
is a man in your kingdom who has the spirit of
the holy gods in him….also the ability to inter-
pret dreams, explain riddles and solve difficult
problems. Call for Daniel, and he will tell you
what the writing means." (Daniel 5:10-12)

Slowly pushing his 90 year-old body toward the palace to
which he was summoned, the pain of his long past teenage
trauma pierced Daniel's heart again. In the enemy invasion of
their homeland, he and his youthful friends were captured out
of their upper class comfort and exiled to the pagan metropolis
of world power. But instead of excitement at such an elegant,
grandiose city, the glamour of it had only grieved them more.

"By the rivers of Babylon we sat and wept
When we remembered Zion.
There on the willows we hung our harps,
For there our captors asked us for songs,
…..How can we sing the songs of the Lord
…...in a foreign land?" (Psalm 137:1-4)

Although this memory flooded him with feelings of national
failure, Daniel forced his mind to focus on the good impact he
was chosen to make on a foreign empire. But as he walked, he
wondered: Why had he been given the gift to decode all the
dreams of Babylonian kings, but not the code God had given to

him by visions, dreams and angel visits? Having been warned to seal it up for the time of the end, he knew his job was to just write down the mysteries. These cryptic communications that he and his contemporaries could not understand somehow held the key to Earth's future.

How could he have imagined that for over 2000 years, people would still be putting together the prophetic pieces of the puzzle of the "Daniel Code"! In far flung future generations, certain clues would only be clear when close to happening, but, even so, the Lord had said "...none of the wicked will understand, but the wise will understand." (Daniel 12:10)

Now, finally being brought into the banquet hall, Daniel wasted no time proclaiming to the now paralyzed party in the palace that the writing meant the king was finished.

His flagrant sins had passed the patience of the Most High and a regime change was already happening. Hadn't Daniel's fellow prophet, Isaiah, written 150 years before what was going on at that moment? Spelling out the character and purpose of this future Persian conqueror, Yahweh had even named him Cyrus long before he was ever born.

In fact, during the very time of Belshazzar's feast, Persian troops had been quietly diverting the course of the Euphrates River. How else could they capture the greatest fortified city without a battle? Sneaking under its immense, impregnable walls on the dried river bed, Babylon was brilliantly taken with only the king being killed.

Mingled thrills and suspense elated Daniel's spirit as it came back to him that this was the very conqueror chosen to liberate the Lord's exiles. Soon a decree would release them to go back and rebuild their ruined capital city, Jerusalem. But after seventy years, how many would want to leave? He wouldn't blame them. Who would want to look at the poor pile of ruins of the most glorious temple in the world, looted of billions in gold?

However, what few could figure out was how its builder, the wisest king of all time, could have ended up a fool making the worst demon idol shrines. Why had such a marrying mania seized Solomon? How did his harem of a thousand pagan women work the wickedness that harnessed his heart to Satan's subversion? God was angry, and from then on it was downhill to destruction for Israel.

Lucifer and his lords loved it when God finally sent the invincible armies of Babylon to destroy His own temple, city and people. They had a vested interest in its downfall and planned to make the most of it!

Looking at it from the perspective of their rival kingdom, they saw it as a reward. Hadn't they done a lot of work through the relentless allure of their sex goddesses, nature fertility gods and zodiac superstars?

From its beginning, the prince of darkness had his dragon eyes fixed on this most fabulous temple. He even threw a parallel dimension party when his agents built the houses of homosexual prostitutes right next to God's new golden house.

But how could even that compare with the triumph of taking his demon deities right inside the temple itself? There they were! Carved and painted on the walls with the esteemed elders of Israel bowing and worshipping them–right under Yahweh's nose! Chutzpah triggeed horror. Then with more men praising the rising sun in the doorway facing east, and women in ritual weeping for the Tammuz god (a Nimrod alias), the devil was delirious with his successful sabotage. It hadn't been easy but now he could sit back and enjoy its total destruction!

For all the years God's prophets had been warning about it in ghastly detail, hadn't he always maintained a large contingent of false prophets in denial? Didn't they keep painting a picture of peace and safety so that almost nobody believed the negative promises of God? Until He finally unleashed them!

Exhilarated at the chance for a new beginning, Daniel's thoughts raced back over the panorama of his people's past. In his mind's eye, he saw Joshua taking over from Moses and conquering Canaan by supernatural strategy...the exploits of the judges...the priests...the kings. Their pinnacle of glory, wealth and fame had only increased spiritual rebellion. How now would the ancient oracles get out to the world? When would the Daniel code be cracked? Only the Most High knew, and he was getting ready to do something that would cost Him everything!

WHITE HORSE FORCE:

Book One

Who Can Make Me a *Super-Immortal?*

PART FOUR

COSMIC BIRTHDAY SPLITS TIME:

THE STORY OF YOUR CHAMPION

13
ANGEL EXTRAVAGANZA

_ᖇᖇ_

The oil wick flared into flame overcoming the darkness, as Miryam (Mary) lighted a lamp on the Hanukkah menorah. In the shadows that shot up the wall, she could almost imagine those huge wine-crazed Syrian battle elephants! How had the small Maccabee guerilla army ever won against them? It could only have been God and that was why she enjoyed celebrating this holiday at the darkest time every year (even though it was not in their scriptures). Mary knew that if Judaism had continued to be banned in Israel by the Greek king of Syria, then Messiah could never come.

But now (around 2 B.C.) everyone was even more urgently looking for His arrival, because the descendants of the Maccabees had betrayed them and their land was occupied by Rome! Still, why should they complain? Didn't they get to observe this festival of dedicating the temple, cleansed of defiling idol statues of Zeus and swine sacrifices? Weren't the Romans giving them freedom for all their other appointed feasts? Yes, but taxes were oppressive, ungodly pagan lifestyles were rampant and everything had to be politically correct with Caesar–or else! As long as religion was kept a private and personal matter only, and government-approved priests were in charge, God would be tolerated.

As all her flashbacks faded in the lamp glow, Miryam remembered to be thankful they were allowed to study the Word of God in their synagogues. Searching the scriptures for clues about the coming Messiah had always fascinated her.

Then all of a sudden, the flickering menorah lights were engulfed in a far greater glow! A shining angel appeared, scaring her out of her wits! Was she dreaming…or having a vision? And what was his shocking greeting about her being highly favored to give birth? The angel, (whose name was Gabriel) told her:

> "…you are to give Him the name Yeshua (Jesus). He will be great and will be called the Son of the Most High. The Lord God will give Him the throne of His ancestor David, and He will reign over the house of Jacob forever. His kingdom will never end."

Astounded, Mary asked him how this could happen, as she was a virgin. The angel's answer left her totally awe-struck! "The Holy Spirit will come upon you, and the power of the Most High will over shadow you. So the Holy Child to be born will be called the Son of God."

At that moment, not daring to dream of the dangers involved, she yielded her whole being, telling the angel: "Behold the handmaid of the Lord; may it be done to me according to your word."[47] After Gabriel left, she could hardly believe it was true. That thousands of years from God's promise to Eve,[48] she should be the woman to receive the sacred Seed! Miryam's mind could hardly contain this concept. And who would ever believe such an impossible thing? As just a teenage girl in the small town of Nazareth in Galilee, Israel, how could she ever expect the young man to whom she was engaged, to accept such a fantastic story? She couldn't. But she had just agreed to submit to God... no matter what! Now a chill ran through her as she grasped what it might cost.

But in heaven, the holy angels were on high alert. Wasn't God's great mystery plan of the ages about to be activated? Would His Son still be willing to carry out the mission agreed upon before the creation of the world? Although He had created everything and knew everything, there was one thing He had no way of knowing: What it would feel like to be trapped inside a human body! Stripped of His resplendent celestial glory and omnipotence, He would humble Himself to enter mortal flesh with an Earth birth![49]

To trick Satan, God planted His Seed in the womb of a VIRGIN! That Seed was destined to be the great victor over the serpent's seed, as He had promised Eve so long ago in Eden. From now on, the Kingdom Wars would rage to the next level (with a lot more surprises for the Devil).

All the angels were ready for their assignments. They loved appearing in dreams to Earth people, and for this event they'd get to do it often. For starters, one would tell Yosef to go ahead and marry Miryam, because her Baby was conceived from the Holy Spirit! However the contingent rehearsing their great spectacular sky celebration was the most excited of all.

It wasn't as if this would be an unheard of miracle. Some 700 years earlier, the heavenly Father had the Holy Spirit dictate these predictions which were then written by Isaiah the Prophet:

> "Behold, the virgin shall be with child and bear a Son, and they shall call His name Immanuel (God with us)"[50]

> "A Child will be born to us, a Son will be given to us...and His name will be called Wonderful Counselor, Mighty God, Eternal Father, Prince of Peace...."[51]

At last, when the nine months of her precious pregnancy were completed, Mary was mystified when Joseph told her they would have to take a trip–due to the Romans. Caesar had issued a decree for an empire-wide census. Everybody would have to go back to their ancestral villages to register.[52]

As they traveled by foot and donkey from Nazareth south to Bethlehem, Miryam (Mary) marveled at the uncanny coincidences of the Creator! Wasn't this the time of Tabernacles, when all of Israel was supposed to "camp out with God" in booths made of branches? Although it was now the final fall harvest festival, they were supposed to eat and sleep for a week looking up at the stars to remember God's miracles of providing their needs for 40 years in the desert after leaving Egypt. Wouldn't that be amazing, she thought, if her divine Baby, "God With Us" would be born at this time![53]

Would He even send some supernatural sign, she wondered, to celebrate this nine month marvel depicting Messiah-sent (Christ-mas)? Perhaps around Hanukkah would be the best time to tell the whole story...since it was the conception that was supernatural, rather than the birth. But, even so, it could become the cosmic birthday that would split time, before and after on many calendars.

Because they were both descended from King David, the young couple was heading to his small city close to Jerusalem. No wonder the Inn was filled up when they got there. Even their relatives' houses were overflowing with pilgrims attending the Sukkot festival.

By now it was night, and all the Innkeeper could offer was his stable filled with the travelers' animals. Mary's labor pains were quickening now, so what else could she could do but lay on the hay and pray? Not far away, shepherds were watching over their flock of holy lambs for temple sacrifice.

Then it happened! As if by an unseen signal, the sky lit up like noon, leaving them dumbfounded and trembling. A huge angel was hovering overhead making a mind-boggling proclamation:

> "Do not be afraid; for behold, I bring you good news of great joy which shall be for all the people; for today in the city of David there has been born for you a Savior, who is Messiah, the Lord. This will be a sign for you; you will find a Baby wrapped in cloths and lying in a manger (animal feeding trough)." (Luke 2:10-12)

Then the whole sky erupted with a multitude of the heavenly angel army praising God and saying:

> "Glory to God in the highest, And on Earth peace among men of goodwill." (Luke 2:14)

Needless to say, the shepherds rushed to the rustic scene, shouting the sensational story to everyone they saw! And over a thousand years later, at the darkest time every year around Hanukkah, the Holy Spirit would impel millions worldwide to sing about the arrival of The Light Of The World![54]

> *"Joy to the world, the Lord has come,*
> *Let Earth receive her King;*
> *Let every heart prepare Him room,*
> *And heaven and nature sing..."!*

> *"Angels from the realms of glory,*
> *Wing your flight o'er all the Earth;*
> *Ye who sang creation's story;*
> *Now proclaim Messiah's birth;*
> *Come and worship, come and worship,*
> *Worship Christ, the newborn king."*

> *"O little town of Bethlehem, how still we see*
> *thee lie;*

*Above thy deep and dreamless sleep the
silent stars go by.
Yet in the dark streets shineth, the everlasting Light;
The hopes and fears of all the years are met
in Thee tonight.*

*O holy Child of Bethlehem, Descend to us
we pray;
Cast out our sin and enter in, Be born in
us today.
We hear the Christmas angels the great glad
tidings tell;
O come to us, abide with us, Our Lord
Emmanuel."*

---

*"Hark! The herald angels sing, glory to the
newborn king!
Peace on Earth and mercy mild, God and
sinners reconciled.
Joyful, all ye nations rise, join the triumph
of the skies;
With th' angelic host proclaim, Christ is*

born in Bethlehem
Hark! The herald angels sing, glory to the
newborn king!

Christ by highest heaven adored; Christ the
everlasting Lord;
Late in time behold Him come, offspring of
the favored one.
Veiled in flesh, the Godhead see; Hail the
incarnate Deity
Pleased as Man with men to dwell, Jesus,
our Immanuel!

Hail the heaven born Prince of Peace! Hail
the Sun of Righteouness[55]
Light and Life to all He brings, risen with
healing in His wings.
Mild he lays His glory by, born that man no
more may die;
Born to raise the sons of Earth, born to give
them second birth.
Hark! The herald angels sing, glory to the
newborn king!"

"Away in a manger no crib for a bed,
The little Lord Jesus laid down His sweet head,
The stars in the sky looked down where He lay,
The little Lord Jesus asleep on the hay.

Be near me, Lord Jesus, I ask Thee to stay
Close by me forever, and love me, I pray;
Bless all the dear children in Thy tender care,
And take us to heaven, to live with Thee there."

"O holy night! – the stars are brightly shining,
It is the night of the dear Savior's birth;
Long lay the world – in sin and error pining,
Till He appeared and the soul felt its worth.

A thrill of hope the weary soul rejoices
For yonder breaks a new and glorious morn:
Fall on your knees, oh hear the angel voices!
O night divine, O night when Christ
was born!"

14
COUSINS AT
THE CROSSROADS

___ꞔꞔ___

Having heard and seen this panorama of enemy angels invading His territory, Lucifer burned in anger, but helplessly watched unable to silence them.

Mockery prevailed among the archons of the atmosphere and their master of malice, the prince of the power of the air. What could God be up to? This so called "King of the Jews" must be a joke! As a Messiah, He would have to be riddled with ridicule. Who would ever believe the Son of God could be a Baby born in a barn? But, just in case, Satan decreed they should speak to the powers that be to cancel this little "King," since they couldn't risk another Moses getting away!

Herod was not happy. Who were these Magi from Mesopotamia claiming some "King of the Jews" had been born, because they "saw His star in the east?" What to do? As the Roman puppet-king in Jerusalem, he could tolerate no rivals, not even an infant Messiah! There was no way but to slay all male babies in Bethlehem born two years before or less. The soldiers of Rome, who largely disdained the Jews anyway, would be up to the heartless task, he knew.

Meanwhile, climbing down from their camels in the town pinpointed by a prophet 600 years before, the Magi found and bowed to Jesus. Didn't their gifts even declare his destiny? Gold (royalty), Frankincense (worship), and Myrrh (suffering). After that, in order to escape Herod's monstrous massacre, the dream angels got busy and told the Magi to detour and Joseph to take Mary and Jesus to Egypt immediately.

Fleeing south through the Sinai, the fateful family were spared the screams rising from the houses where the Roman slaughter of male children was happening... but Satan had missed the One intended!

Arriving in Alexandria, Yosef (Joseph) soon found work in the street of the carpenters. He and Miryam (Mary) and Yeshua (Jesus) were thankful to settle down among the large Jewish community of exiles in Egypt. But how long would they have to stay there? Mary didn't want to feel impatient, but ever since Joseph had consummated their marriage (after

Jesus was born), she was eager to go home and start the rest of their family.

Finally, another dream angel announced they were free to leave because the king who sought the Child's life was now dead. Nearing Jerusalem, they heard another horrible Herod had taken the throne, so they headed back up to Nazareth. Although that name meant "Branch," it would be a long time before they realized the ancient oracles had written of the Messiah being "The Branch."[56]

Growing up in Galilee, He who was the Architect of the Universe and Builder of the House of Israel, learned carpentry from His Earthly supposed father. By suffering and testing in a poor human family, He learned humility and obedience.

At age 12 however, He could no longer resist the flashes of His divine nature that were breaking through. The large company of parents, relatives and friends He had traveled with to the yearly Passover festival in Jerusalem suddenly found Him missing on their way back. After a frantic three day search of the city, Yosef and Miryam finally found Yeshua in the temple.

Surrounded by stunned rabbis and experts of the law, He seemed to be conducting his own Bar Mitzvah! (coming of age ceremony) "...sitting among the teachers, listening to them and asking them questions. Everyone who heard Him was amazed at His understanding and His answers."

When rebuked by His parents, He said, "Why were you searching for Me? Didn't you know I had to be about My Father's business?" At this point, Mary and Joseph were clueless and couldn't understand what He was talking about. It wouldn't be the last time they would lose sight of who He really was.[57]

Knowing a priest or rabbi was not allowed to teach in public until age 30, Yeshua grew up with his half brothers and sisters, developing patience and discipline in submission to His parents. But often, He would get homesick for heaven and go up on a mountain to commune with His real Father.

At last the day came! Jesus started traveling south to the Judean desert, determined to do whatever it would take to accomplish His Father's assignment for this urgent Earth mission. Hadn't he already heard there was a great quest in the air out there for Messiah to emerge? And who was that strange man clothed in camel hair, shouting for people to change, and immersing them in the Jordan River near Qumran? It was the first prophet of God after 400 years of silence, and everybody knew John the Baptizer was speaking the Word of the Lord!

Yeshua, of course, knew exactly who Yohanan (John) was. Born only six months apart, the two cousins both grew up with much gossip surrounding the weird, supernatural circumstances of their mothers' pregnancies. One was a teenager who claimed to be a virgin bearing the Son of God! The other was an old childless woman, perhaps 65 or 70, married to an even older priest, when she gave birth to a baby boy. Both said an angel had announced the impossible, and why should anyone in Israel doubt either of them, since the whole nation was descended from Laughter (Yitzhak), the son born to a 90 year old mother and 100 year old father!

Then, suddenly spotting Yeshua coming among the crowd toward him, John declared, "Behold the (sacrifice) Lamb of God who takes away the sin of the world!" Now everyone's eyes were fixed on Jesus as He walked into the water to receive his symbolic Mikveh (immersion of purification). As He came up, the sky opened and the Holy Spirit descended on Him in the form of a Dove, as a heavenly Voice spoke, "This is My beloved Son, in whom I am well pleased."[58]

For starters, the Holy Spirit had agreed to send Him to a strange rendezvous. It was a desert mountain confrontation with the ex-top angel, Lucifer, whom the Son of God Himself had not only created but thrown down out of heaven like lightning. Having failed to kill the right Baby, Satan was now waiting to take his challenge to the next level. Originally, the manifesto spoken in his heart was only to be LIKE the Most High. But now, having eavesdropped on Gabriel's pronouncement to Messiah's mother, he wanted more!

Beyond all celestial imagination, he was now ready to ask God to bow down and worship HIM! Having outwitted the wisest king ever (Solomon), Satan's insane arrogance was now sufficient to confront the King of Kings. But Jesus, though weak and hungry after fasting forty days in the wilderness (like Moses), simply and coolly brushed off this outrage by speaking scripture:

> "Be gone, Satan
> for it is written, 'you shall worship
> the Lord your God and
> Him only shall you serve.' " (Matthew 4:10)

What was to be the great reward offered for worshipping Lucifer, the failed angel? All the kingdoms of the world... which Yeshua already had power over anyway...if He chose to take it before the appointed time. Actually, the greater temptation at the moment was when Satan said, "If you are the Son of God, command these stones to become bread." Hadn't He felt a surge of victory over those gnawing pains in His stomach when wielding His word-sword back with:

> "It is written, man shall not live by bread
> alone, but by every word from the mouth of
> God." (Matthew 4:4)

Now Yeshua knew Satan had become more deranged than ever. The longer he believed his own lies, the worse it got. So after Jesus ate and drank what His Father's angels brought Him, He returned in the power and anointing of the Holy Spirit, eager to set the devil's captives free! [59]

15
SNAKE ON A POLE

—⟨∂⟨∂—

Trudging through the dusty desert back toward the green of Galilee, Yeshua always seemed to be full of surprises. In the first place, why was he born in a stable? Why did the angels not announce His birth to the religious establishment? Why was He now collecting His future ambassadors from among ordinary fishermen and even despised tax collectors for the Roman overlords? Clearly, a new and radical paradigm was happening here.[60]

Strangest of all, why had His forerunner, cousin Yohanan, proclaimed Him as the Messiah and then declined to follow Him? Why did some of *his* disciples leave him for Jesus, while others thought there was a competition going on? Why hadn't John himself and his whole group just gone over to Jesus? Mysteriously, John had put himself into a different classification based on Messiah's future wedding banquet guest list! Saying that the Bridegroom has the bride but that his assignment was as the friend of the Bridegroom...sort of a best man or groomsman. Apparently, a spiritual line was about to be drawn between the House of Israel and what was in the process of becoming the House of Messiah! Did it look like a split might be shaping up between the hard liners of Moses and what Yeshua was now calling "new wineskins?"[61]

John (Yohanan) had been living dangerously. Having denounced the king (Herod) for illegally marrying his brother's wife, she eventually asked for his head on a platter. While imprisoned in the dungeon of a desert fortress, John even began to doubt the identity of Jesus, sending some of his disciples to take a message back to Him:

"Are You the One who should come, or should we look for another?"

After answering with a list of the miracles He was performing as evidence, Yeshua added a cryptic twist...

"....and blessed is he who does not take offense at Me."

"...among those born of women, there has not arisen anyone greater than John the Baptizer, yet the one who is least in the kingdom of heaven is greater than he."[62]

But as it was soon to be seen, His cousin would not be the only family member to forget or reject His real identity.

However, His Name was now like a magnet. Crowds were converging from everywhere in the region and across borders from neighboring countries to see Him. Yeshua from Nazareth; Rabbi, Holy Man, Healer, Miracle Worker, and maybe even Messiah! Wherever they heard He might be, people made a bee line for the area. At one point, many thousands were climbing a grassy hill by Lake Kinneret–the Sea of Galilee. There they all were dusty, dirty, sweaty, and exhausted, having walked many miles carrying their little ones. But they were desperate to be set free from disease, demons, hopelessness and oppression. Looking at them as lost sheep that nobody cared for, Jesus' heart was moved with great compassion. Wasn't this why His Father had sent him here?

As a Master storyteller, He would keep people intrigued and perplexed by His parables for three days and then multiply a few morsels of food to fill up more than 10,000 before sending them home. But only to the disciples who traveled with Him, who had left everything to follow Him, did He give complete teaching. No doubt many were mystified by His methods as He educated His entourage which shockingly included women. When He was alone with His own He explained everything saying, "The secret of the kingdom of God has been given to you" (but not to outsiders).[63]

Of course Satan knew his turf was being invaded and his captives being set free, but he was working on a plan through his agents in the religious supreme court to pull off an inside job. Meanwhile, why were demons freaking out and shrieking out and blowing His cover everywhere Jesus went? Knowing exactly who He was, because He had created them as angels eons ago, they were terrified, speaking out of the people they possessed saying "...have You come to destroy us before the time?" Usually, Yeshua would just shut them up and cast them out....and then their victim would suddenly become a normal, healthy person again.[64]

Gratefully, in profound wonderment, the people were exclaiming, "We've never seen anything like this. With a word He casts out evil spirits." However, in their jealousy, this didn't stop the religious elite from actually accusing Yeshua of being demonized Himself and doing His miracles by Satanic power! After pointing out the absurdity of Satan dividing his own kingdom by casting himself out, Jesus exposed the real identity of His attackers and sealed their doom.

> "You belong to your father, the devil, and you want to carry out your father's desire. He was a murderer from the beginning...there is no truth in him...he is a liar and the father of lies." ...whoever blasphemes (insults)

the Holy Spirit will never be forgiven; he is guilty of an eternal sin."

He said this because they were saying "He has an evil spirit."[65]

Those He had continually been calling hypocrites had now passed the point of no return. Knowing there were only two sources of supernatural power, they had picked the wrong one in Yeshua's case. After He had healed a man who had been BORN blind (a test sign of the Messiah), they were without excuse. Now they would be positioned on God's celestial chessboard to carry out the plan to sacrifice His Son...His Lamb!

Although Yeshua had come as the Champion of the children, nobodies, outcasts and misfits...not all of the super religious were hostile to Him. In fact, there were many who believed who He really was but kept it secret, "because they loved the praise of men more than the praise of God." Jesus taunted them, saying "...the prostitutes and tax collectors come into the kingdom before you do."[66]

When one of these leaders, Nicodemas, quietly sneaked in to see Him at nighttime he got an electrifying earful! To begin with, Messiah told him that unless he got born again from above by the Spirit, (not reincarnated in a flesh baby), he could neither see nor enter the kingdom of God. Then He summed up His entire mission to planet Earth:

"No one has ever gone into heaven except the
One who came from heaven – the Son of Man.
Just as Moses lifted up the snake in the desert, so
the Son of Man must be lifted up, that everyone who
believes in Him may have eternal life.
For God so loved the world, that He gave His
only begotten Son, that whoever believes in Him shall
not perish but have eternal life.
For God did not send His Son into the world to
condemn the world, but to save the world through Him.
Whoever believes in Him is not condemned, but
whoever does not believe stands condemned
already...This is the verdict. Light has come into the
world, but men loved darkness instead of light because
their deeds were evil."[67]

Or, as Yohanan the Baptizer had told his disciples when
they asked him about "that Man," "Whoever believes in the
Son has eternal life, but whoever rejects the Son will not see
life, for God's wrath remains on him."

Israelis scanning the springtime hillsides surrounding the
Sea of Galilee saw the romantic return of the rainbow wild-
flowers as a breathtaking sight! Using these love tokens He
had created to prove His care for people, Jesus was telling
His followers not to worry about material things:

"See how the lilies of the field grow…If that
is how God clothes the grass of the field…
will He not much more clothe you? Seek first
the kingdoms of God, and His righteousness,
and all these things will be given to you…
Do not store up for yourselves treasures on
Earth…but store up for yourselves treasures
in heaven…for where your treasure is, there
your heart will be also."[68]

Then, always puncturing the postures of the pompous,
Yeshua stifled the self-importance of His disciples by hugging little children. The disciples asked, "Who is greatest in
the kingdom of heaven?" And He said, "Unless you change
and become like little children, you will never enter the
kingdom of heaven. Therefore, whoever humbles himself
like this child is the greatest in the kingdom of heaven. See
that you do not look down on one of these little ones. For I
tell you that their angels in heaven always see the face of My
Father in heaven" [69]

Yeshua's teaching style was tantalizing to many Israelis
because He spoke with absolute authority and not like their
rabbis, who only quoted each other. For instance, He was
furious about their invented traditions which heaped impossible burdens of religious rituals that He said were making
the Word of God void. God's basic commandments were lost
like a needle in this holy haystack of man-made legal trivia.[70]

In contrast, Jesus was saying to them:

> "Come unto Me, all you who labor and are
> heavy laden, and I will give you rest. Take
> My yoke upon you and learn of Me for I am
> meek and lowly of heart and you will find
> rest for your souls. For My yoke is easy, and
> My burden is light."

On one hand, He was offering them relief from the
unnecessary layers of laws smothering the law given to them
through Moses; but then on the other hand He was suddenly
going way beyond it, up to an ultimate level they hadn't yet
dreamed of!

> "Love your enemies and bless those who
> curse you, do good to those who hate you and
> pray for those who despitefully use you and
> jump for joy when men speak evil of you and
> persecute you for My name's sake, because
> great is your reward in heaven."[71]

After imparting power to 70 of His disciples, Yeshua sent
them out to do the same miracles He was doing. Coming
back elated at their success they said, "even the demons are
subject to us in Your name!" Continuing His crash course on
the kingdom, Jesus told them not to rejoice about that but to

rejoice because their names were written in heaven. After all, He had seen Satan fall from heaven like lightning. Telling them that Satan comes only to steal, kill and destroy, He said, "I have come that they might have life more abundantly."[72]

Life on the road was wearing, and whenever Jesus and His inner circle were nearing Jerusalem, they greatly enjoyed the hospitality of His close friends, Mary and Martha and their brother Lazarus in Bethany. Always, it was a welcome oasis on their continual journey to savor a dinner there. But in making the meals, Martha was fastidious and Mary was oblivious...sitting rapt at Yeshua's feet, immersed in His teaching. Then, reversing women's required roles, He refused to concede that kitchen chores were more important than scripture study. He told Martha when she complained that, "Mary had chosen the good part and it won't be taken from her." Was this a preview of radical changes for women in His coming kingdom?[73]

Everywhere Yeshua and His disciples went, crowds from the whole region would discover their whereabouts and swarm around Him to be healed. Because of this, trouble was brewing on the home front. His half-brothers didn't believe who He was, so friction in the family was inevitable.

> "When His family heard about this, they went to take charge of Him, for they said, "He is out of His mind." Then Jesus' mother and brothers arrived. Standing outside they sent

someone in to call Him. A crowd was sitting around Him and they told Him, "Your mother and brothers are outside looking for You." "Who are My mother and My brothers?" He asked. Then He looked at those seated in a circle around Him and said, "Here are My mother and My brothers! Whoever does God's will is My brother and sister and mother."[74]

Why did Yeshua snub His flesh family? Because He was intent on building a new faith family: Not the House of Israel, or the House of Jacob, or the House of David, but the House of Messiah! Hadn't He already told them He didn't come to bring peace but a sword that would separate family members? Also, if they didn't love Him more than their wives and children, mothers, fathers, sisters, and brothers, they were not worthy of Him. They were to deny themselves, take up their cross daily and not love their lives in this world or else they would lose eternal life with Him in the Kingdom of Heaven. He was not of this world, His kingdom was not of this world and they were to be not of this world also. Everyone who hated and insulted Him would hate and insult them because of His Name. In this world, they would have trouble, but they were to be joyful because He had overcome the world and was giving them His peace in their hearts, which would surpass all understanding.[75]

Now, somebody came with a message that His good friend, Lazarus, was sick. The twelve members of the inner circle were shocked that Jesus just stayed put. Even when word came that Lazarus had died, He waited four more days (because He was planning a spectacular miracle and knew that the religious experts did not consider anyone totally dead until that length of time had passed).

Arriving in Bethany, Yeshua's group met with Mary and Martha and the large assembly of friends, relatives and religious leaders from Jerusalem who were observing the days of mourning for Lazarus. Although they were all saying (truthfully) that if Jesus had been there, he would not have died; they were clueless about what was going to happen next.

Yeshua told them, "I am the resurrection and the life..." He asked to be taken to the tomb. On the way there, everyone was sad and heavy hearted and Jesus, feeling their sorrow, wept too. After He requested for the stone to be rolled away from the cave burial place opening, Martha said, "But, Lord, by now he stinks!" Jesus reminded her that He had told her she would see the glory of God, and then shouted. "LAZARUS, COME OUT!!"

The dead man came out... Jesus said to them "Take off the grave clothes and let him go." Therefore, many of the Jews who had come to visit Mary, and had seen what Jesus did, put their faith in Him.[76]

Because Yeshua was the Champion of the common people and mingled with them to show compassion on the "lost sheep," the religious snobs called Him a glutton and wine drinker and friend to sinners. But He told them that the "children of the bride chamber" couldn't fast while the Bridegroom was with them, but they would later, when He was taken away.[77]

Controversy about the kingdom was ringing in the air everywhere! Why did this arrogant, uneducated young Galilean who claimed to be not only Messiah but also God, keep them all in suspense? Didn't He know how they were all suffering under Roman occupation and urgently needed for Him to take over? As the Son of God, why wouldn't He perform a stupendous wonder of deliverance like Moses at the Red Sea? After all, most of the Hebrew prophets had pictured Messiah as a great conquering King, destroying Israel's enemies...and they were writing the words of the Lord Himself!

Jesus had turned water into wine at a wedding, raised the dead, walked on the sea, healed lepers, and made a man born blind see, and other creative miracles unheard of before–but the leaders were calling for some supernatural sign out of the sky! Oddly, He gave that very prediction to His inner circle, but told the religious establishment "the kingdom is within, or among, you." What was this puzzle of some sort of inside-out kingdom that starts in hearts, but then, at some future point in time, zooms out of heaven like lightning down to Earth?[78]

As the whole nation began preparing for the annual Passover week festival, Yeshua seemed to be rushing toward a dangerous climax. As a rebel against the status quo, He was expert at verbal hit and run, knowing it was necessary to avoid getting Himself killed before the appointed time. Even the hometown folks in Nazareth had tried to throw Him off a cliff for puncturing their ethnic pride, so He had learned quickly how to disappear in a crowd.[79]

Displaying as much tenderness toward the downtrodden as He did fury to the hypocrites, He stumped His critics with brilliant comebacks and sardonic humor that left them speechless! Seeing and hearing His showdowns with clergy and demons of disease, the crowds gasped, "He does all things well."

They were ready to praise Him in a palm branch parade down the Mount of Olives shouting, "Hosanna (Save Now), Blessed is He that comes in the name of the Lord."

Didn't they know this would make the Romans nervous? Even though He was only riding a humble donkey (predicted by the prophet Zechariah 600 years before), they knew that palm branches were the royal symbol of victory for Messiah-King.[80]

Now what was that crashing noise coming from the temple courtyards? Running inside, the disciples could hardly believe it; Jesus was in a rage with a whip! Coins clattered everywhere as He kicked over merchants' tables shouting for them to get their wares out of there. "Is it not written, 'My House shall be called a House of Prayer for all nations?' But you have made it a robber's den." Often, Jesus' followers were shocked at His extremes, but they were soon to become totally undone by the outrageous intensity of His love.[81]

Meanwhile, in another dimension, the ancient Dragon was decidedly irate! Summoning the full court of his Kingdom to an emergency brainstorming session, the Devil was desperate. Pacing in his palace, he was ranting about how his kingdom was being ravaged by this God-Man and His Apostles, driving his demons out of people all over the Holy Land. His worst day ever was when an entire legion of his dutiful demons was evicted from a violent, deranged wild man, who then suddenly became normal.

But why did Yeshua have to grant their request to go into a nearby herd of swine? All the pigs panicked and plunged into the lake! Now all these homeless devils were complaining and nagging him to do something about it. But they all knew it was no use, seeing Lucifer staring daggers at them.[82]

Urgent questions swirled in his malevolent mind. How could he evade that Eden prophecy? Was this Jesus the "Seed of the woman" predicted to crush his head? How could he make sure this Super-Exorcist would be executed before He could impart His power to any more people to do the same things He was doing? Not to worry; as always, money and fear would provide the solution. This much Satan knew: The religious hypocrites were in his pocket because they couldn't continue to co-exist with a wonder-working Messiah exposing them by Truth. If He suddenly set up His kingdom, they would all be out of their jobs!

Now things were looking up. The stage was just about set. His infernal informers had noticed potential in one of the 12 apostles. Judas was a money loving thief, freely stealing from the bag of offerings people were giving to Jesus. Betrayal would be just the next logical level…if the price was right. Naturally, it would be an inside job (Satan's favorite strategy).

The brutal Romans, of course, would not be a problem. Wasn't their famous killing machine what had always held the great empire together? "Pax Romana" prevailed by blood and taxes. Everyone knew that and Lucifer was convinced he could count on it when he needed it most. The god of this world system would win again (or so he thought).

Every year, as the Most High had commanded, all of Israel, inside and outside their land, relived the Passover escape from slavery. In Jerusalem, thousands of perfect lambs lined the lanes leading to the place set for their sac-rificial slaughter–the Holy Temple. As always required, their blood would be splattered on the altar, the priests and the people. Just as in Egypt, it was one lamb for a house-hold. Only now, instead of rushing out into the unknown, the families would stay in their houses to recall the whole story. Eating the lamb in leisure, they reclined on cushions to emphasize their freedom. Slaves done dine and recline!

But what did the Lamb of God have planned for the last Seder with His 12 closest friends? Did they yet know why He had to die? Not really, although they had heard Him loudly proclaim: "No one takes My life from Me. I have power to lay it down and power to take it up again." However, little did they dream that that most fateful night would be the beginning of mind-boggling revelations to revolutionize the world![83]

Unlike the days of His youth when he always enjoyed the Passover Seder with His natural family, this night was to be different from all other nights; beginning a new type of celebration with Yeshua's spiritual family. As the 12 gathered with Messiah in an upper room, tension was building. The Romans, famous for their legendary feats of engineering of roads, aqueducts, stadiums, racetracks and theatres, were also the innovators of unique dining arrangements.

The triclinium, so called, was a low U-shaped table surrounded by couches. With one elbow propped on the table, the guests could indulge in the ultimate luxury of lying down while eating. Inside the U, a server would freely move with a steady supply of food and drink, while the diners could lean back on each other for more intimate conversation. Typical of the time, a more affluent Roman menu might have included exotic appetizers like jellyfish and fungi, and main courses such as flamingo tongues, wild boar and lobster with truffles and ending with pastries and fruit.

Strangely, in order of table seating, Jesus had put Judas, whom He had called a devil, in the place of honor right next to Him! On the other side was Yohanan, brother of Yaakov (John and James), whom Yeshua had dubbed "sons of thunder." But the youngest and most beloved of his inner circle of Peter, James and John had always been John.[84]

That final evening, questions, answers, new teachings and amazing promises were flowing fast back and forth between the bewildered disciples and their departing Lord and Master. As they ate the roast lamb, unleavened bread and bitter herbs to recall Israel's ancient escape from Egyptian bondage, Yeshua suddenly changed the meaning of the ritual!

> "And He took bread, gave thanks and broke it, and gave it to them, saying "This is My body given for you; do this in remembrance of Me." In the same way, after the supper, He took the cup, saying "This cup is the new covenant in My blood, which is poured out for you."[85]

What was this strange idea of Messiah giving Himself as a new covenant? Why did He then quote the Biblical engagement speech to betroth a bride? But the statement that astounded them all was Jesus' emphatic exclamation of exclusiveness: "I am the way and the truth and the life. No one comes to the Father except through Me."[86]

Although these twelve ambassador disciples had grown accustomed to being startled by things Yeshua did and said, He now did something they would never have guessed. Taking off His tallit, Jesus started acting out a slave ritual. After tying a towel around His waist, He knelt and dealt with each friend the same; washing their feet in a basin of water and drying them with the towel. Peter, their impetuous leader, protested. But how could any of them at the time grasp this prophetic picture of how His future body was to perform with this humility in the world?[87]

Abruptly, suspense grabbed the group as Jesus grimly announced that one of them would betray Him. Noting it was necessary so He could fulfill what had been written long ago, He said that for the one doing the betrayal, it would have been better for him to never have been born. Then indicating it was Judas, Yeshua turned and told him to do what he was going to do quickly. Already, Satan had entered into Judas and he made his way to the religious rulers and collected the thirty silver coins agreed upon for the blood money.[88]

Walking forlornly across a deep valley to a garden on the Mount of Olives across from Jerusalem, Jesus said to the disciples, "My soul is overwhelmed with sorrow to the point of death." Turning away, He fell with His face to the ground and cried out to His Father three times that, if possible, this cup (of suffering) might be taken from Him. Yet, in the end, each time He submitted, saying, "Yet, not My will but Your will be done."

What exactly was it that caused His Spirit and flesh to recoil in such agony that it even made His sweat bring forth blood? Was it only the dread of crucifixion, or was there something more–something invisible and unimaginable? But before the Earth was even created, He had agreed to His Father's request to do this, while not knowing at all how it was going to feel.[89]

Did the mystery have to do with that strange snake on a pole lifted up by Moses that Yeshua said He would have to re-enact? Way back during Israel's exodus from Egyptian slavery, God got so furious at their constant kvetching (complaining) while He was miraculously keeping them alive in the desert, that He sent a plague of snakes through the camp, killing thousands! When Moses desperately pleaded for mercy, the Lord told him to make a brass snake, lift it up on a wooden pole and proclaim that anybody who looked up at it would be healed and live. In a way, that was a future forecast of how Satan, that ancient serpent of Eden, would be defeated by the Seed (offspring) of the woman, while bruising His heel (on a cross).[90]

Interestingly, in more recent centuries, Satan had been advertising himself as a healer. Switching the snake as a symbol of sin to a symbol of the sun, his logo became a serpent-circled disc which had long been all the rage in Rome.

In fact, snakes had reached the peak of popularity as pagan pets! In almost every house, the "sacred serpent" was to be found. "These serpents nestled about the domestic altars," said the author of POMPEII, "and came out, like dogs and cats, to be patted by the visitors, and beg for something to eat. At the table, they crept about the cups of the guests, and in hot weather, ladies would use them as live boas, and twist them around their necks for the sake of coolness. These sacred animals made war on the rats and mice, and thus kept down one species of vermin; but as they bore a charmed life, and no one laid violent hands on them, they multiplied so fast that, like the monkeys of Benares, they became an intolerable nuisance. The frequent fires of Rome were the only things that kept them under control."

But how did this craze catch on so fast and continue so long? Actually elite educational institutions had convinced people that it was the path to ENLIGHTENMENT. After all, wasn't it the ancient serpent/devil/dragon who, in Eden, had made mankind "in the know" (Gnostic), by acquiring knowledge of both good and evil? It was no mystery how these religious mystery systems had arrived in Rome. They were a long range gift from Babylon. Hundreds of years earlier, when Persian conquerors kicked out Belshazzar and his Chaldean priests, they fled west to the kingdom of Pergamon (now in Turkey).

With a warm welcome from the king they set up shop there, creating a famous shrine of the "man instructing snake" (Aesculapius)...which they celebrated with the most frantic orgies. After establishing their college in the region, the Chaldean priests began training the locals in psychic occult divination and all science, real or pretend. Later, when a colony of Etruscans from the area migrated to the north of Rome, they brought their supernatural skills in Babylonian mysteries along with them.

It wasn't long before, out of respect for their powers, the highest of the noble youth of Rome were being sent up to Tuscany to be instructed in the sacred science. Then the pagan Roman Pontifex began carrying as his standard, a fire-worship snake (appropriately colored) on top of a high pole!

Now what connection was all this going to have with Messiah's mode of execution? Hadn't He originally been announced to be the LAMB of God? Who in Israel had ever seen a lamb nailed to a cross? Certainly no one. They all knew that the Passover lambs were killed painlessly. But what they also knew was that it was the criminals who got crucified (as well as political enemies)! Of course, the Romans had crucified thousands of men, and not too long before, the Jews had even done the same to some of their own people. Decadent descendants of the heroic Maccabees had crucified 800 holy men (Pharisees)!

The awesome difference with Yeshua the Messiah however, was that He was the only one in history who had ever VOLUNTEERED! In Lamb-like quiet submission He was surrendering Himself to the violent death of a criminal. In earlier times, God had instructed the Israelites to hang criminals on trees as a curse. But now, He had determined to submit His only Son to this ultimate shame. How else could the sin debt of the human race ever be paid? God had long considered them all to be spiritual criminals. Nevertheless He was desperate to redeem them; to buy them back out of slavery to sin, self and Satan.[91]

Now was the time. The enemy was closing in. Judas betrayed his Master with a kiss as the signal to the soldiers he had led up to the garden. As Jesus had predicted all His disciples fled in fear and deserted Him. Taking Him bound to the house of the high priest at night, the whole religious court there was getting frustrated with the conflicting evidence to convict Him. Finally, after He refused to answer all the accusations, the high priest demanded point blank, "I charge you under oath, by the Living God: Tell us if you are the Messiah, the Son of God." " I AM," said Jesus, "And you will see the Son of Man sitting at the right hand of the Mighty One and coming on the clouds of heaven."[92]

Knowing this to be a reference to the Daniel code and He was claiming to be the Son of God, the high priest proclaimed it blasphemy. The verdict was death. Then they began to spit at Him, striking Him with their fists, slapping and mocking Him. As dawn was breaking through the sky, the top religious establishment led Yeshua bound to the Roman governor, Pontius Pilate.

After listening to their long list of angry accusations against Him, not the least of which was that He claimed to be Messiah the King, Pilate was stunned that Jesus stayed silent. The governor asked Him, "Are you the king of the Jews?" "Yes, it is as you say," Jesus replied. Normally, Pilate had no problem having people executed for various reasons, but this day he was perplexed and apprehensive, not finding any clear cause for a death sentence. Also, while he was sitting on the judge's seat, his wife sent him this message, "Don't have anything to do with that innocent Man, for I have suffered a great deal today in a dream because of Him."[93]

Why had the Jewish court brought Jesus to the pagan Romans for trial anyway? Hadn't they always retained power to try and execute religious offenders such as this one who they had convicted of blasphemy for claiming to be God while still a Man? The problem was public opinion. They had to find a political reason to convince the Romans to condemn Him quickly at night so when the great crowds of His followers found out, they could pass the blame. But this plan turned out to be not so easy, as Pilate kept resisting their crucifixion demands. He said, "Take Him yourselves and execute Him."[94]

Going back inside the palace, Pilate asked Jesus, "Are You the King of the Jews?" Jesus said, "My kingdom is not of this world...if it were, My servants would fight...but now My kingdom is from another place." Thinking it would satisfy their fury, and avoid execution, Pilate handed Jesus over to his soldiers to be whipped. But what spirit was gripping them now to turn into agents of torture, going far beyond the usual flogging? Was Satan seizing this chance to try again to kill Him before His hands and feet could be pierced, as the prophets had written?[95]

Beating and punching Yeshua as they laughed and mocked at His claim to be King of the Jews (which to them was the equivalent of "King of the Nothings"), the soldiers of the great world empire twisted a crown out of long thorn branches. They jabbed it into His head while spitting on Him and pulling out his beard. The result was a bloody mess that hardly looked human. Then they went to work with the whip. Made up of leather strands studded with chunks of bone, glass and metal, it was designed to strip away the flesh into ribbons and slash through muscle tissues until organs would hang out of the body.[96]

Saying again that he still found no basis for a charge against Him, Pilate brought out Jesus, lacerated, mutilated, with a purple robe and the crown of thorns. Still, the priests and their officials shouted, "Crucify, Crucify! We have a law and according to that law He must die because He claimed to be the Son of God." This made Pilate more afraid and he asked Jesus where He came from. Then he tried even more to set Him free. But the Jewish leaders finally played the Caesar card. Shouting, "If you let this Man go, you are no friend of Caesar. Anyone who claims to be a king opposes Caesar." Pilate said, "Here is your king. Shall I crucify your king?" But they shouted, "Take Him away, take Him away! Crucify Him! We have no king, but Caesar!" Finally, Pilate handed Him over to them to be crucified. Then the soldiers took charge of Jesus, who carried His own cross to a place called the hill of the skull.[97]

A sharp, shining knife in the priest's hand flashed as he swiftly slit the lamb's throat. Its blood poured into a bowl. It had been painless. That day in Jerusalem, thousands of perfect Passover lambs were sacrificed at the temple. This was a merciful method ordained by God for the innocent animal sin-substitutes. But not so for His Son. Outside the city gates, there was another Lamb...a Man Lamb...the Lamb of God sent to take away the sins of the world. Heavy iron spikes were hammered through his wrists and ankles onto crossed wooden stakes. It was not painless. Nobody dreamed that this "serpent on a pole" would become the eternal emblem of salvation and healing to the ends of the Earth. Unseen, above the cross, twelve legions of angels were hovering, just in case Yeshua changed His mind. His enemies scoffed, "He saved others – let Him save himself and come down from the cross, and we will believe in Him." The angels knew it was taking far more courage for Him NOT to come down...and fail the assignment His Father had given Him from the foundation of the world. Because His executioners didn't understand the mission on which He was sent, He said, "Father, forgive them, for they don't know what they are doing."[98]

When His blood poured down on the Holy Land, Yeshua was giving Himself as the New Covenant which He had promised. This unique Blood of God could never simply renew any existing covenant, but would become the DNA of a whole new global nation called "The Body of Messiah." As the agonizing, crushing weight of humanity's most vile sins was bearing down on Him, Jesus' Heavenly Father had to turn away in revulsion at the ghastly, hideous sight. This was His worst moment of all and He cried out what his ancestor, King David, had written in prophecy a thousand years before, "My God, My God, why have You forsaken Me?"[99]

But while He was despising the shame, and the soldiers were gambling for His clothing, Jesus suddenly visualized the joy set before Him: His future offspring now being mysteriously birthed in travail, an uncountable multitude from every tribe, tongue and nation seated with Him in heaven at His marriage feast in resplendent glory! No matter what it took to birth it, it would all be worth it. The glorious bride bought by the blood of the precious, spotless Lamb-Man. Extravagant, irrational, unfathomable love was pouring out beyond time and space to draw all who would come into a New Creation…to be set free from sin, self and the kingdom of Satan.[100]

While two criminals had been crucified on either side of Him, they were not of interest as the onlookers continued to revile and ridicule Jesus for the outrageous claims He had made about Himself...especially since Pilate had a sign in three languages fastened to the cross reading "JESUS OF NAZARETH, THE KING OF THE JEWS."

After all, everybody knew that no righteous rabbi or wise master teacher or even a miracle working prophet would ever claim to be what this Man had. . . to have come down from Heaven where He existed eternally as the Son of God! No simple good man would ever say such things. Either he was a liar or a lunatic or really who He said He was. There were no other options. Nobody had ever talked the way He talked...or done the things He had done...least of all the founders of various religions.

At a distance, many women who had followed Yeshua from Galilee to provide for His needs were watching in horror and grief. But closer to the cross stood His mother and beloved disciple, John. As a High Priest of Heaven offering Himself as the ultimate sacrifice, Jesus proclaimed, "It is finished," (paid in full) and, bowing His head, He gave up His spirit into His Father's hand. What was His Father's response? God plunged the whole land into darkness for three hours (noon to 3 p.m.) and ripped the thick heavy, towering tapestry temple entrance curtain from top to bottom, like the ancient prophets tore their clothing in mourning. Also the Earth quaked and the rocks split and the soldiers watching gasped in terror gasping "Surely this was the Son of God"![101]

Because the religious officials could not leave bodies on crosses on a holy day, they asked the Romans to speed up the death process by breaking the legs. Seeing that Yeshua was the only one already dead, instead of breaking His legs the soldier pierced His side with a spear, causing blood and water to pour out. Just as the first Passover lambs at the exodus from Egypt could not have a bone broken, so it was written of God's Lamb, "not a bone of His would be broken." But what would happen to His body? All dead bodies of criminals were thrown over the wall of the steep cliff supporting the temple mount. Far below in the Kidron valley, was a perpetually burning trash dump, a relic of child sacrifice to fires inside idols, which Jesus had used as a metaphor of hell.

But one of His wealthy secret followers, Joseph of Arimathea, persuaded Pilate to give him the body and he and Nicodemas wrapped it in linen with spices and laid Yeshua in his own new rock cut-tomb in a garden...and the women were watching.[102]

16
FIRSTBORN FROM THE DEAD

L ike a billion electrons, intense light shot from every cell of His corpse, searing the shroud with a photographic negative as Yeshua burst from his burial bindings! Now He had business in Tartarus. Diving down into the depths of Earth's core at the speed of thought, Jesus streaked like laser lightning in his new unique super-body. As the echoes of His victory shouts reverberated down to the lowest prison of the abyss, news of Messiah's subterranean invasion spread like the fires that were tormenting millions of mortal spirits.

Heralding and proclaiming His triumph over death, hell and the grave, He crushed Satan's head under His heel, which still had the hole of the wound that bruised it. Now what were those unbearable wailings from the dungeons of the extreme depths of the pit...the special off-limits chamber called Tartarus? Thrashing their gigantic chains against invisible walls, the Titans writhed and howled in darkness so thick it seemed gripping. As the most evil of Lucifer's rebel angels, they had come down to seduce Earth women, producing races of wicked giants before the global flood. Blasting through the gate of the abyss, Yeshua grabbed the keys of death and hell from Abaddon (Apollo), the destruction angel, while compelling every knee under the Earth to bow, and every tongue to confess that He was Lord, to the glory of God the Father! [103]

Then the Savior of the world let the Nephilim know that His Father had appointed Him to be the supreme Judge of all the living and dead, and that the Lake of Fire had been prepared for them and their dragon master.

Joy at Jesus' crucifixion had quickly turned to agony in the underworld, as He openly humiliated the princes of darkness in Satan's kingdom. After Messiah's raid in Hades, the god of this world was forever judged guilty and his eternal sentence pronounced...but he would not yet be incarcerated...only "out on bail" to see how many more foolish humans he could delude for the final showdown. Now that the Champion of those miserable Earth dwellers had won the victory for them, Satan would see how many he could keep from finding it out! But hadn't the great deceiver always deceived himself most of all? So he convinced his angels that they would still have some pawns in the planetary chess game. One thing about demons, however, there were no atheists among them. They believed and trembled, knowing their eternal doom. Although serving the evil one, they weren't fools since it was written the fool has said in his heart "there is no God."[104]

Zooming across the vast canyon of separation, Jesus at last escaped the stench of hell to visit the resting place of the souls of believers long waiting for His arrival in comfort with Abraham. Speaking LIFE! He suddenly sent thousands up from the grave in brand new bodies! It was at this point the great faith of Job was rewarded who had written 2000 years earlier:

> "For I know that my Redeemer lives, and that
> He shall stand at the latter day upon the Earth;
> and though after my skin worms destroy this
> body, yet in my flesh shall I see God..."[105]

Popping back up through the planet's crust as if it were butter, Yeshua walked out right through the huge stone sealing the entrance of His tomb. But in order to expose the empty interior of the burial chamber, two angels came and rolled back the stone to show that there was no body inside, only a shroud full of spices.

As pink dashes of dawn pushed against the darkness, two women both named Mary, made their way toward the tomb of Messiah. It was very early the first day of the week, the day the Romans had named after their sun god. But what was that sun-like splendor now entering their eyes? Looking up in awe, they saw it emanated from an angel sitting atop the huge rolled away stone!

Seeing that the inside of the tomb was empty, Miryam from Magdala began weeping, thinking Yeshua's body had been taken away. When Jesus Himself suddenly showed up, she failed to recognize Him and thought she was asking the gardener where he had laid His body. But when He spoke her name, Mary Magdalene whirled around, exclaiming RABBONI, and clung to Him. Rabboni. Master. Teacher. Lord!!! It really was Him! How could she not be ecstatic that the One who had cast seven demons out of her was truly, incredibly, back from the dead! She was elated beyond belief. The impossible had actually happened!

But Yeshua had to hasten to heaven to His Father, and He left her with a message to take to His disciples. Gratefulness began growing in her heart to envelop her entire being. For a woman there wasn't even supposed to be a Rabboni, Master, because all the other teachers allowed only men to be their disciples. But Yeshua was radically different. Both Miryam of Bethany and Miryan from Magdala and others had sat at His feet, hanging on to His every word. Of course, this unheard of situation generated plenty of gossip, and Jesus hated how Satan would use it to twist the truth and poison people's minds for millennia. But because He urgently needed everybody—men, women, and children, to run with

His good news message worldwide, He gladly broke the traditional taboos of His time.[106]

Meanwhile, havoc had hit the Roman guards. They were terrified and dropped down when an earthquake hit and an angel that looked like lightening rolled away the sealed stone. Not only was Jesus' tomb empty but many holy people came up out of their graves and walked around Jerusalem appearing everywhere.[107]

The heavy iron bolt clanked as it snapped into place; locking the eleven closest companions of Yeshua behind the door of their upper room hideout. Terrified by fear of arrest by the same religious court that condemned the Messiah, they huddled in the place where that last perplexing Passover Seder had happened. But now, it seemed like months ago, even though it had only been just three agonizing days! How were they going to figure out this whole horrendous catastrophe? Weren't they required to mourn for the dead, saying specific prayers for at least seven days?

Hearing the secret code knock, they jumped up nervously and peeked through a crack in the door. It was Mary Magdalene, leading an elated envoy of women, pushing her way in and shouting wildly that she had seen the Lord Jesus ALIVE! Strangely, the disciples refused to believe her, or the others, probably thinking they had seen hallucinations or a ghost. Peter and John however, did run to the tomb and saw that it really was empty, with only the cloths still lying inside.[108]

Finally, the suspense was ended when, not much later, they were all back in their locked room and Yeshua Himself simply showed up, announcing the traditional peace greeting "Shalom Aleichem!" Of course they were scared, thinking it must just be His Spirit, because, after all, what else could walk through locked doors and thick walls? But He said, "Why are you troubled and why do doubts arise in your hearts? See My hands and My feet? That is I Myself. Touch Me and see, for a spirit does not have flesh and bones as you see that I have."

He rebuked them for not believing the women, but seeing they were overjoyed and still incredulous, Yeshua asked if they had anything to eat. Having just finished their dinner, they offered Him a piece of broiled fish and some honeycomb. As He ate, He began teaching them and opening up their minds to understand all the predictions which were written centuries ago about him in the Law of Moses and the Prophets and the Psalms of the Holy Scriptures. [109]

After Yeshua disappeared again, the disciples were overflowing with joy and mind-boggling new revelations. But then they suddenly thought, "What next?" Hadn't they given Him three years of their lives? Didn't they leave their homes and families to walk the weary roads with Him? What now? They were clueless.

Remembering that He promised they would sit on twelve thrones in His Kingdom, judging and ruling over the twelve Tribes of Israel, they wondered how that would happen now.

Of course they were beyond astonished and excited about Messiah appearing alive from the dead, but who knew when or even if He would show up again? All His instruction on ancient prophecies about His death had been fascinating but the suspense for His Kingdom was getting confusing. So why not just go back up to Galilee and return to fishing on the lake? To Peter and John, it seemed like a good idea.[110]

Beach breakfast for the overnight fisherman was really like dinner at dawn. Straining to see the foggy figure on the distant shore, they soon knew something supernatural was going on. After catching nothing all night, they reluctantly followed the stranger's advice to throw their net from the opposite side of the boat. Instantly, the net nearly burst with the large fish. Then John said to Peter, "It is the Lord." Landing the boat, they saw He already had a charcoal fire with fish grilling on it and also some bread. After serving all seven of the disciples who were there, Yeshua's eyes penetrated into Peter's soul and spoke of some of the unfinished spiritual business that had to be taken care of before He could leave planet Earth. [111]

Among the group of around 500 disciples still faithful, word went out to meet the Lord on the Mount of Olives near Bethany on a certain day. Only the twelve had heard His future plans at the Last Seder, the night before He was crucified. Now they were all converging, perhaps for the last time, on the flowery sprinkled hillsides of their favorite camping grounds. Suspense and confusion mingled on most faces but what they were about to see and hear would startle and challenge them far beyond anything yet imagined.

> Then Jesus came and spoke to them saying, "All power (authority) is given unto Me in Heaven and in Earth, therefore, go and make disciples in all the nations, baptizing them in the name of the Father, the Son and the Holy Spirit, teaching them to obey all the things I have commanded you. Go into all the world and preach the good news to all creation and these signs will follow those who have believed: In My Name, they will cast out demons, they shall speak with new tongues and they shall lay hands on the sick and they shall recover."[112]

Although riveted to His words, many of the disciples were feeling frustrated about this message. Wasn't it all backwards? Hadn't they always heard the opposite? It wasn't supposed to be like this. Didn't all the prophets paint pictures of Messiah redeeming Israel, ruling on his throne in Jerusalem, and all the other nations coming up there to worship and be taught by Him? How could He tell them to take His message to the whole world when Jewish laws prevented them from even entering the house of a pagan, much less eating with them? Not only that, but they remembered hearing Him say He was sent to the lost sheep of the house of Israel, although He also had made a cryptic remark about having to bring "other sheep that are not of this fold." [113]

Finally, they just had to ask Him directly, "Lord, will You at this time restore the kingdom to Israel?" He said to them, "It is not for you to know the times or season which the Father has put in His own authority." Then commanding them not to leave Jerusalem until they were baptized in the Holy Spirit in a few days, Jesus said they would be clothed with power from on high, which was the promise of His Father. But before they could start wondering just what this mystifying experience would be like, Yeshua lifted His arms to pronounce a blessing over them. Before He was finished speaking, they breathlessly watched Him rising up in the air! [114]

Vanishing into a cloud, His friends were left staring, astounded, into the wild blue yonder. Finally, two angels appeared to grab their attention and convince them of Jesus' future comeback!

> ...and suddenly they saw two men dressed in white standing next to them. The men said, "You Galileans! Why are you standing staring into space? This Yeshua, who has been taken away from you into heaven, will come back to you in just the same way you saw Him go into heaven." (Acts 1:11)

155

Now, a deep peace began rising in their spirits as they remembered Jesus' promise at the Last Supper, that He was going to prepare a place for them and would return to take them to Himself so that where He was they would be also!

The air was electric with excitement and anticipation as they made their way down the steep path of the Mount of Olives. Even the familiar, narrow stone streets of Jerusalem now seemed to glow with the glory of Messiah's fantastic promise! [115]

WHITE HORSE FORCE:

Book One

Who Can Make Me a *Super-Immortal?*

PART Five

PROMISE DRIVEN WIFE:

The Story of Your Hope For Glory

17
POWER FROM THE
MOST HIGH POWER!

_϶ϲ_

Jerusalem was jammed with Jewish men making pilgrimage at Pentecost. All over the city the feel of a festival was in the air, as they joyfully navigated the rigors of ritual at the ancient Holy Temple Mount. Since the God of Israel required them to meet with Him at three appointed times each year, they were glad and grateful for the Roman roads and Roman peace (Pax Romana) which enabled them, as expatriates, to travel safety.

Did perhaps any of the populace feel a few twinges of remorse for what had happened to the holy Man, Yeshua of Nazareth, 50 days ago at the previous feast of Passover? Despite all the quashed rumors about His tomb being empty, would God let them forget about it, or was He planning a spiritual cataclysm?[116]

Miryam yawned. Wedged into a window seat, she felt the spring night chill still clinging to the cobblestones, begin to be burned off by the early summer sun. Others, at the other upper story windows wondered if her Son's promised mystery would manifest now at Pentecost. Still surprised at the new status Jesus had given them, she and the other women were part of the 120 in the house for the whole ten day prayer meeting. Then all of a sudden out of nowhere, a roaring, rushing hurricane hit right behind her, nearly knocking her off her seat! But the weird thing was outdoors was all calm and sunny, while this hurricane was happening inside the house! And while flames of fire hovered over their heads, a group of Galilean peasants became instant international linguists…fantastically fluent in languages they never learned.

Curious crowds were coming closer, all claiming the same strange experience. "Why are each of us hearing these people proclaim the glories of God in our own native tongues? We live everywhere from Iran, Iraq, Turkey, Egypt, Libya, Rome, Crete, and Arabia." But others were mocking, saying, "These men are just full of sweet wine!" That did it. One of them would have to seize this matchless moment! Although three years ago when Jesus had chosen them, most of the twelve disciples were teenagers. Peter, now twenty-something liked to take the lead. Transformed suddenly by the Holy Spirit from wimp to wild, he stood up to proclaim a bold message, confounding those who thought Jesus was dead and gone. "Fellow Jews and all of you who live in

Jerusalem, let me explain this to you... These people are not drunk as you suppose...it's only nine o'clock in the morning! No, this is what was spoken by the prophet Joel:"

"In the last days, God says, I will pour out My Spirit on all people. Your sons and daughters will prophesy, your young men will see visions, your old men will dream dreams. Even on My servants, both men and women, I will pour out My Spirit in those days, and they will prophesy. I will show wonders in the heaven above and signs on the Earth below, blood and fire and billows of smoke. The sun will be turned to darkness and the moon to blood before the coming of the great and dreadful day of the Lord. And everyone who calls on the Name of the Lord will be saved." (Joel 2:28-32)

But what is the actual name of the Lord? In the Biblical book of Proverbs it was written "Who has established all the ends of the Earth? What is His name and His son's name?" Now Peter was about to shock them completely with the answer!

"Men of Israel, listen to this: Jesus of Nazareth was a man accredited by God to you by miracles, wonders and signs, which God did among you through Him, as you yourselves know. This man was handed over to you by God's set purpose and foreknowledge; and you, with the help of wicked men, put Him to death by nailing him to the cross. But God raised Him from the dead. Therefore let all Israel be assured of this: God has made this Jesus (Yeshua), whom you crucified, both Lord and Messiah."

Convicted and cut to the heart by the spiritual power pouring from Peter's mouth, the crowd felt desperation descending as they cried out: "Men and brothers, what shall we do?" "Repent" replied Peter, "turn your lives around and all of you be baptized in the name of Yeshua the Messiah for the forgiveness of your sins, and you will receive the gift of the Holy Spirit. Be saved from this corrupt generation!" By the day's end, the total number of souls immersed to receive the promise actually totaled 3,000![117]

Far above, but not too far, the two angels from Jesus' tomb and ascension were leading more than a million other angelic guardians in a singing and dancing celebration unseen in the sky. A late arrival to the scene interrupted to ask, "Why all this lavish extravagant jubilation?" Stopping their praise for just a moment, two angels answered in tandem: "Because Michael and Gabriel just reminded us of the awful tragedy on this same day 2,000 Earth years ago when the law of Moses being given resulted in 3,000 being killed. But today, the Spirit was given and 3,000 were saved!"

As the last man was sinking down deep into the purifying pool of the Mikva, a vision flashed through his mind's eye.

Being an Egyptian Jewish pilgrim, he well remembered the history of the golden calf crisis. Before Moses could even come back down the mountain with the ten laws of God, the people were already busy breaking the first two! Incredibly, they were indulging in an idol orgy for one of the demon gods that the real God had destroyed by the ten plagues He sent on the land of Egypt. Then the terror of the Lord had flashed like fire as He commanded those loyal to Him to kill the idolaters with swords (even their own relatives!).

But now a new age had dawned, and after Peter and John had healed a lame beggar at the temple gate through the Name of Jesus, their powerful preaching led 5,000 more to believe. So these 8,000 became the nucleus of a new nation, bought and birthed by the blood of their own rejected and crucified King. Though as yet unaware, this unique assembly was destined to go global...and ultimately, even cosmic! But first, they needed to find out from the Holy Spirit, just who and what God had recreated them to be.[118]

18
THE NEW CREATION NATION

⟶ ⟶

All of a sudden, the followers of that crucified holy Man, hated by the hierarchy, had exploded from a few hundred to 8,000 and counting in only a few days. Jerusalem was overflowing with baptisms in His Name. Holy Spirit house huddles were happening all over the city to hear Yeshua's teachings and to daily break the bread and drink the wine, re-enacting the New Covenant He had made in His blood. This was to remain the defining ritual of the Body of Messiah for time immemorial.

All over the Holy City, the sick, the sinners, the misfits, the desperate, hopeless and those oppressed or rejected by organized religion, came crowding to the miracle message in the streets. Signs, wonders and demon deliverances were spreading like wildfire from the fingers of Yeshua's followers. There was no way their enemies would not notice.

So because multitudes of both men and women were constantly becoming believers in the Lord Jesus, jealousy enraged the high priest and his supreme court so that they grabbed his ambassadors and put them in the public jail. But who knew that God was about to orchestrate a supernatural prison break?

> "...during the night an angel of the Lord opened the gates of the prison, and taking them out he said, 'Go, stand and speak to the people in the temple the whole message of this Life.'" (Acts 5:19,20)

Early the next morning, as the high priest and whole senate of Israel was gathered for the trial of the prisoners, the officer found they had vanished, even though the prison was locked up with the guards still at the doors. Then hearing the disappeared prisoners were back again teaching people in the temple court, officers were sent to quietly bring them before the Council. When the high priest again ordered them not to speak in this Name, Peter and the apostles boldly announced: "We must obey God rather than men!" Though persuaded by a reasonable rabbi not to furiously kill them on the spot, the high priest did have them all flogged.[119]

Now their backs were bloodied with excruciating pain from the 39 whip lashes, but nevertheless the 12 brothers in

Messiah left the Council "rejoicing to be counted worthy to suffer shame for His Name."

Another young man, however, was not so reasonable as his former rabbi, and as an agent of the high priest was determined to drag the "Nazarenes" to oblivion. Saul was a spiritual terrorist! Working for the religious establishment that had murdered Messiah by proxy, he swore to destroy His followers also. Ravaging their assemblies, he entered houses, dragging out both men and women for torture, prison and execution.

> "Now Saul, still breathing threats and murder
> against the disciples of the Lord, went to the
> high priest and asked for letters…to the syna-
> gogues at Damascus so that if he found any…
> he might bring them bound to Jerusalem."
> (Acts 9:1,2)

But heaven had others plans. Before they could enter the city, a Light brighter than the sun at high noon flashed intensely around Saul, knocking him to the ground. What could this superior solar Light possibly be? Could it even be that Primordial Light which created the sun on the fourth day? Frozen in fear, Saul's mind frantically searched the scriptures stored in it. Hadn't he trained to be a Pharisee from age three, memorizing them seven hours a day? But now he was at a loss, as a Voice began speaking out of that blinding radiance:

> "Saul, Saul, why are you persecuting Me?"
> "Who are you, Lord?" he asked. "I am Jesus whom you are persecuting, but get up and enter the city...." (Acts 9:4-6)

Due to his notorious reputation, a local disciple that Yeshua had appeared to was more than reluctant to visit Saul. But being told that he had nothing to eat or drink for three days and was praying, still blind, Ananais relented and agreed to go and lay hands on him. When this happened, the scales fell off Saul's eyes, he received the Holy Spirit and was baptized in Yeshua the Messiah. And he ended up joining those he had come to arrest!

Hard as it was for many disciples to believe that Saul had switched sides, they dropped their doubts when he began boldly debating in the synagogues that Jesus was the Son of God. So it wasn't long before the Jews who were hostile hatched a murder plot against him; watching for him at the city gates day and night. Everyone knew that Damascus was a most ancient, completely walled city, with all the gates guarded, so Saul was wondering what possible plan of escape his newfound friends could come up with?

Curling up in the bottom of the big basket, Saul cringed to hear its creaking ropes scrape the stones of the city wall while being lowered at night by his courageous companions. For the first time in his life, Saul was glad to be small! This escapade would never have worked for a larger, heavier man. Actually, he didn't care anymore that his Greek name, Paul, meant "little," especially since God had just assigned him a destiny of great things!

With a desperate prayer for invisibility to the guards, Saul crawled quickly out of the basket, and clutching his bag of provisions ran toward the vast, velvet blackness outside the city. One thing he knew for certain: He must go nowhere near Jerusalem! By now, his former associates were sure to have reported him as a traitor who had defected to that crazy cult of the crucified Messiah. Also, he knew that Yeshua's disciples would have a very hard time believing that. Yearning for another encounter with the Living God above all else, Saul set out to see Mount Sinai, 200 miles to the south in Arabia, seeking something like Moses and Elijah the prophets had thousands of years before. Would he also see the volcanic fire or hear the still, small voice? However, never could Paul have imagined that this rendezvous would result in a revelation to transform the world for all time![120]

19
PETER'S PARADIGM SHIFT

———৩৹৹———

"Arise, kill and eat!" boomed the Voice from heaven. Peter, praying on a rooftop while waiting for lunch, had fallen into a trance. Up in the sky above the ancient seaport town of Jaffa on the Mediterranean coast of Judea, an unthinkable vision was appearing; a huge sheet hovered full of non-kosher animals forbidden for Jews to eat. What could God be thinking to command such a thing? Was the law of Moses being changed or superseded? Heaven forbid! But the Voice said, "What God has cleansed, no longer consider unholy."

"Not so, Lord," pleaded Peter, "nothing unclean has ever entered my mouth!" But the Voice and vision were repeated exactly the same two more times, totally perplexing Peter until he was startled by visitors knocking and asking about him at the gate downstairs. Ordinarily, he wouldn't have anything to do with the three pagan men wanting to know if he was staying there, but the Holy Spirit already said He had sent them and to go along without trying to figure it out. As he was about to discover, it was a supernatural set up.

After asking the reason why they were there, the men replied, "We have come from Cornelius the centurion. He is a righteous and God-fearing man who is respected by all the Jewish people. A holy angel told him to have you come to his house and give a message." So Peter invited them to stay overnight before setting out up the coast for Caesarea. At this point, who could guess the spiritual shock awaiting them all at this Roman soldier's house?

Meanwhile, a day's journey to the north, Cornelius was pacing past the massive stone aqueduct arching across the sand of the deep harbor city. Still stunned by his angel visitation, even this commander of over 100 of the awesome army of Rome was finding it hard to prepare for the holy man he had summoned. Striding slowly through the market he could feel the fear following the people's reaction to his uniform. Understandably, the trappings of his authority made an instant impact. Seeing the sideways horsehair crest on the helmet, the chain mail and leather armor, the medals displayed, and the superior quality of the famous red cloak, everyone knew that his rank had been achieved by bravery or military efficiency. In the Italian cohort of 800 soldiers, his status was assured. Spiritually, however, he was about to make history unawares!

Sampling some bread and olives as he placed a large order at the baker's shop, Cornelius was cordially greeted by some passing local rabbis. A surge of gratitude swept over him, recalling the ignorant idolatry and confusion of his youth. "Thank heaven I could visit the synagogues to find out about the Living God who created everything," he thought while walking past the temples of Roma and Caesar Augustus (now considered a god). "I could have been trapped in that popular Persian cult of Mithras, like so many of my soldiers, worshipping in caves with sacred bulls and not even having any scriptures at all!

"No wonder I was always searching for something else," he recalled. "The gods I grew up with, being bigger than humans, just did more evil on a larger scale!" Then, thankfully meditating on Moses' manuscripts, he realized, "How else would I have been enlightened to spiritual reality? How liberated I felt after finding out that these gods were just demon princes who, as rebel angels of Lucifer, mated with Earth women, producing a race of giant demigods called Nephilim." As an evening sea wind caught his cloak, Cornelius felt a shudder of revulsion sweep through his spirit, feeling only a facet of the fury of the Creator's hatred of idols. Those lying competitors were stirring holy jealousy by stealing His creatures' love due only to Him alone. They had hijacked His worship and given it to demons instead.

By the time Peter arrived at his door, the electric thrill of suspense Cornelius was feeling overflowed to the point where he bowed down at his feet. Peter protested "Stand up! I am only a man myself." But then he explained to the large gathering "You are well aware that it is against our law for a Jew to associate with a Gentile or visit him. God had shown me that I should not call any man impure or unclean. I now realize that God does not show favoritism but accepts people from every nation who fear Him and do what is right." What strange spiritual set up was going on here? Peter asked why he was sent for and Cornelius said an angel had requested it, but neither one was told why!

So although he said they already knew it, Peter launched into a review of the story of Jesus and ending with, "He is the One whom God appointed as judge of the living and the dead. All the prophets testify about Him, that everyone who believes in Him receives forgiveness of sins through His Name." Right then a loud interruption rippled through the assembly, stopping the speech. The disciples were dumb-founded. It sounded like God wouldn't wait another minute and was pouring out the Holy Spirit on these ex-heathens. Fantastical languages were flowing from every mouth in the house!

"But how can this be happening?" pondered Peter's party, "These people aren't even Jewish!" Is the Lord making some radical change? Whatever it is, He seems to be in a hurry! Even as Jews, we still had to wait and pray in the upper room for ten days, but eight years later, this roomful of Romans gets it instantly! Why the rush? Is it really time to head, as

Jesus said, for the uttermost parts of the Earth?" Somehow that command seemed more scary now that the unexpected had taken them all by surprise.

Sure enough, scandal had erupted as soon as the news of the forbidden visit spread through the community of Jewish believers in Yeshua. Not until Peter recounted all the details did they calm down after he concluded with: "Who was I that I could withstand God?" Still it was easy for Peter to understand how they were feeling. For as long as he could remember, their own land of Israel had been occupied by non-Jewish foreigners and ruled by the swords of overlords. This new wild thing God had started would take some getting used to. Was He going to end up merging believers in all nations into a new form of humanity?[121]

20
SURPRISES AT
HEAVENLY HEADQUARTERS

Ascending up through the dense cloud of demons surrounding Earth, Peter's angel accelerated to a flame of fire streaking through the cosmos. Laughing all the way, he could hardly wait to take his heaven break and share the news of the Spirit-transformed Jews! Being given permission immediately upon arrival by the Archangel Michael, Peter's angel began reporting his story to the whole assembled celestial army.

"It all happened around Passover. The religious rulers had Peter put in prison under heavy guard. But that very night, I went in (invisibly of course), and jabbed him awake, making his chains fall off. Then as I led him out through the streets of Jerusalem, Peter thought he was dreaming it all, until I left him at the house where they were holding a prayer meeting for him. When he rang the bell, it was so funny because this little girl named Rhoda came running but was too excited to open the door when she recognized Peter's voice. After she went back and told all the others who it was outside the gate, they thought it must be me, his angel, instead of him! Humans are so hard to fathom! They get together and pray for a miracle, but when it happens, they can't believe it! How odd is that?"

Next, following angelic protocol, Peter's angel wanted to ask a favor of Michael, the great archon Prince protector of Israel. Often, the missions of Michael and Gabriel would bring them into territorial conflict with the Prince of Persia and the Prince of Greece over their cosmic domains. Because of the immense size of this awesome warrior, Peter's angel approached a little nervously, asking "Is it all right if I just stay a little longer up here at Home Base? I'm craving a glimpse of the progress on the vast Banquet Hall." When Michael nodded, Peter's angel unfurled his wings just for fun and zoomed to another part of planet Heaven. Then he floated and hovered over the rainbow banqueting banners, peeking down at the panorama of preparations ongoing for the future feast.

Just below, legions of wingless server angels were setting miles upon miles of the most lavishly appointed tables ever dreamed of! Located between the Throne and the country-side, this wedding hall of Heaven was continually enlarging as more names of Earth dwellers were added to the guest list (the Lamb's Book of Life). Though by invitation only, the Father had been planning this for His Son for ages, but most of those summoned were too busy with mundane distractions to accept. They thought the exclusive door into it was too narrow for their lifestyles and just assumed that when the time came they would somehow figure out a way to crash the party. But the Son (Yeshua) had already warned that they would crash and burn instead.

Hearing a familiar "WHOOSH," Peter's angel knew before he even turned around, that a legion of watcher angels had just arrived back from planet Earth. Swiftly surrounding him over the entrance to the vast pavilion, they were all suspenseful about the same question. "Please tell us, what do you think? Could this be where Yeshua the King will drink the mysterious 4th cup at last?" We remember that you and all the angels of the other apostles were at the last Passover supper when he stopped at the 3rd cup!"

As they all settled in on the soft jade glowing green grass under a jungle canopy resonating with curious, comical creatures, Peter's angel leaned on a living water three tier rock fountain, relishing his role as revealer of insider information. "How could I ever forget that fateful night when all of us, the Apostles' angels, heard Jesus speak the promises of a unique heavenly future! Needless to say, we were all horrified when we saw Satan enter into Judas, who fled from the feast to betray Yeshua. But you, of all angels, should remember how

He followed the ancient custom and pattern of Biblical wedding protocol."

Folding his arms and raising his eyebrows for dramatic effect, Peter's angel leaned forward and pointedly pronouncing his premise, exclaimed, "Actually, it was to be the beginning of a blood-stained romance! As you all know, the Passover feast itself was to celebrate anew every year their national rescue from 400 years of slavery in Egypt by putting the blood of a lamb on the doorposts of their houses. So when Yeshua, preparing to offer Himself as the Lamb of God, picked up the 3rd cup of wine, He made it personal in His own blood. Everyone at the Seder table that night must have been more than startled when He said, 'Drink from it all of you, for this is My blood of the new covenant for the forgiveness of sins.'

"As everyone knows, we angels don't have blood. So those of us who fell for Lucifer's lies about himself being the real God were forced to obey him as slaves. Hurled down from heaven like lightning, he morphed into Satan, the Dragon enemy of all God's Creation on planet Earth. Now drafted to deceive humans, his atrocious army of angel rebels all became 'the gods, craving human blood!'" "Oh, don't remind us!" moaned a chorus of watchers. "We're so tired of these never-ending dragon-demon wars that have gone on for eons. Even though we angels who remained faithful to the Most High far outnumber them, they have found many more human accomplices on Earth who think evil is more thrilling than good!"

Sighing in sad agreement as he surveyed the celestial scene, Peter's angel decided to focus on the future instead. That was easy, as his gaze glazed the gleaming edges of the rippling rainbow "huppah" canopies seemingly streaming off into infinity. Stretched between endless columns of stately royal palm trees, this immense pavilion of indescribable splendor filled him with overflowing joy, bringing Psalm 16:11 to mind. "In His presence is fullness of joy. At His right hand are pleasures forevermore."

Just then, a voice from his angel audience, sounding a little impatient, blurted out "Yes, but we still want to know what happened to the traditional 4th cup at the Last Supper!" "Oh, sorry!" apologized Peter's angel, "I got a little carried away. Remember that Jesus told them He would not drink the fruit of the vine from now on 'until I drink it new with you in the kingdom of heaven?' He promised to prepare them mansions in His Father's House and then come again to take them up where He is. Don't all of us know that His Father's House can't be anywhere but up here in planet Heaven? So, the secret of the 4th cup is that Yeshua Messiah couldn't drink it on Earth after the 3rd cup of Redemption (finished by the blood of His cross), because He had to wait for the great wedding banquet in the kingdom of Heaven! That's why He told His followers to reenact the moment of the 3rd cup sacrifice often to 'remember My death until I come.'

This mysterious unique ritual of the bread of His Body and the wine of His blood became the communion shared everywhere among all His faith family."[122]

After hearing all this, a great cheer went up, resounding throughout the whole huge angel assembly. "Wonderful! Hallelujah! We're so glad to hear the rest of the story!" one angel proclaimed. "This is where the suspense of the 4th cup is solved! At the King's great wedding feast for His Son and all of us angels who issued a lot of invitations on Earth, will get to be up here in attendance at the most exquisite event of all eternity!" "Amen!" echoed Peter's angel. "It's been in the planning stages since before the foundation of the world waiting for the Blood of God to buy a global bride, birthing the new creation humanity, destined to become the super immortals needed to rule Earth in the ages to come."[123]

Off toward the Throne in the north, rainbows of living color, flashes of lightening and rolls of thunder beckoned them all to bow down for the Creator of the universe. Afterward, the wide wall of watchers perched on the plush plateau, waved goodbye and simply disappeared. Feeling slightly puzzled, Peter's angel quickly realized they had gone to join the warrior angels providing safe passage past the foul demonic atmosphere encircling Earth. "Why not just immerse myself in the moment," Peter's angel thought to himself, and soak up enough of this all pervasive harmonious living music up here to tide me over until my next visit?" As all the flowers glowed and danced to the myriad melodies, a sudden hidden scene caught his eye.

"What was that?" Peter's angel whirled around to glimpse again a valley stretching beyond a just opened gate filled with neat rows of...could it be...stables? Sure enough, a luminous white horse was approaching him, led by a chuckling worker angel with brushes stuffed in his apron. Immediately intrigued, he had to investigate, even if it meant overstaying his leave of duty. "Are there more of these magnificent white horses in those valley stables?" he demanded. "PLEASE, please," pleaded the celestial stables caretaker, his face shifting from silly to stern. "I must swear you to secrecy! You can't tell Peter or any Earth people yet. We're not allowed to talk about this until the set time for the Most High to reveal it to His chosen servants."

Turning to leave with a cryptic wink, the stable angel started laughing, singing and whispering to his horse as they descended into the greenest of valleys. But as they seemingly pranced in tandem, he called back over his shoulder and recited a little riddle:

> "As the increase of the tables,
> So also is the stables"

As cute little creatures climbed up on Peter's angel, he pondered this clue. Then, oops, a phalanx of fellow angels flew in to escort him back down to Jerusalem where an emergency council was brewing due to trouble in the Antioch assembly. Hurriedly heading to the massive stone wall looming up ahead, they all paused in perfect position at its heavy wood and iron gate. But Peter's guardian, being an apostolic angel, was acknowledged immediately by the 30 foot tall gatekeepers. As they opened the huge portal by a mere hand gesture, Peter's angel and his entourage exited onto the glorious golden bridge spanning a high mountain gorge.

Although they all knew this shining bright bridge of solid gold was where many souls attempted to enter, it elicited an eavesdropped memory from the early days. Peter's angel personally recalled how "I shuddered that day when I overheard Yeshua say to Peter and His other companions; 'Not everyone who says "Lord, Lord" will enter the kingdom of heaven; but he who does the will of My Father. Many will say to Me in that day, "Lord, Lord, did we not prophesy in Your name, and in Your name cast out demons, and in Your name perform many miracles?" Then I will declare to them, "I never knew you, depart from Me, you evil doers." Turning to leave with a last glance at the gleaming bridge, Peter's angel sighed, "Yes, the quest for immortality ends here."[124]

21
TURN THE WORLD UPSIDE DOWN

───⟨⟩───

Streaking swiftly through the dense, gem-like star scape, Peter's angel knew he was needed urgently on Earth. A new drama was erupting on the stage of that tiny blue/green planet; God's theater of the universe! Alighting onto the soil of Syria, he heard about trouble brewing in the Antioch assembly...something about separate tables. And wouldn't you just know his very own assignment person, Peter, was in the thick of it, being publicly rebuked by Paul for hypocrisy!

It seems that before a delegation arrived from the exclusively Jewish congregation of Jerusalem, all the believers, now called Christians, were happily eating together like a newly blended family. But now Paul was livid: He said to Peter "You are a Jew, yet you live like a Gentile and not like a Jew. How is it then that you force Gentiles to follow Jewish customs?" "I live by faith in the Son of God who loved me and gave Himself for me. If righteousness could be gained through the law, Christ died for nothing!"[125]

Taking a break from this religious debate, Peter's angel convened in the clouds with the Antioch leaders angels. "A council of the elders and Apostles is being called to discuss and settle this problem in Jerusalem. Let's all head down there now to exert our influence since we know the Lord doesn't want the Pharisees to win. After all, how could the whole world want the love gift of salvation by Yeshua's cross if they have to first convert to Judaism, be circumcised and do the dietary and whole law code of Moses?" Speaking in their own unique and diverse tongues, all the angels agreed together as they slowly hovered over the Holy City at twilight, just when all of Jerusalem's stones glowed golden!

Emerging from the private tent of his tallit prayer shawl, James (Yaacov) looked stern and concerned. As his fingers felt the fringes and knots of this ancient garment, he felt deeply grateful for the gift of this clothing code the Lord had given to remind them of His laws. But as Yeshua's half brother, Yaacov, he would be asked to change the need for those laws. As it often did, his mind magnetically pulled a picture of his Brother into focus, forcing feelings of unforgettable shock and awe as when He appeared in that resurrected Body.

It had turned his life upside down and now he was leader of the Jerusalem congregation! Sometimes, waves of remorse would overwhelm him for the sarcastic remarks of unbelief he had hurled at Jesus, and wounded his conscience. But what boy could ever understand that the seemingly normal older brother he grew up with was actually God in the flesh? It was a mystery beyond comprehension! Now, as he awaited the arrival of all the apostles, he prayed for wisdom from the Spirit of that unique Brother.[126]

After everyone had come and the greetings were over, what he had dreaded started happening. Yaacov tried to mediate, but when the former fishermen faced the Pharisees, faith fights followed. Everyone knew that Judaism was defined by the law of Moses, given by God to Israel. But now, if the rest of the nations could get in on their promises and their Messiah, without Judaism, wouldn't that be like creating a new religion? Nevertheless, none could deny Paul's report of multitudes of Greeks embracing the Son of God, regardless.

Finally, when Peter protested that the law of Moses had been an unbearable yoke to them and their ancestors, pleading that they not burden the new gentile believers with it, James ruled that a letter listing essentials should be prepared. Choosing several of the other leaders to go with Paul and Barnabas, they all agreed on what the Holy Spirit led them to write about; meat, blood, idols, and sex.[127].

Leaving the Antioch assembly after hearing the letter read, groups of young companions were having lively conversations with some of the elders while walking the covered collonades of the four mile main street. "We had heard," exclaimed one young convert, "that followers of Jesus have to give up sex outside of marriage, but now will we still get to eat pigs?" Laughing at this ex-pagan's equation, an elder answered, "only if all the blood is drained out, they weren't strangled and hadn't been sacrificed to the demon gods on a heathen temple altar...like the local groves of Daphne or sanctuary of Apollo."

As all the young men protested saying, "Well, we have turned from idols to serve the Living God." One could not resist asking; "But why are all religions connected with blood, sex, and food?" After the pretense of offended rebukes by his friends calmed down, the elder patiently explained, "Because those are the three elements of life, or, as Satan would have it–death!" Then just as he was about to remind them of the diet change after Noah's flood, a deafening noise startled them to a standstill.

"Speaking of blood, I hope this roar of rioting sports fans doesn't get anyone killed in the streets again," one of the young men shouted to be heard over the mob. How well they all knew that the whole Roman world was obsessed with chariot races. Two major rivals, the Greens and the Blues were right there in Antioch. Known as the "Queen of the

East," it was the third largest city of the empire, with 300,000 citizens and 200,000 slaves.

"Come on!" called the elder, "Let's head out toward the opening of the new silk road from China!" Grabbing each other's arms, the group slithered like a chain through the crushing crowds, hoping to make it to the massive city walls. As the fading noise level convinced them they had escaped from danger, everyone stopped to praise Yeshua and tie up their togas for speed.

"So obviously," continued the elder, "sports are the real god of this city and the patronage of emperors, and goddesses is just its support network." "True," agreed the young men, "but this is nothing compared to the so-called sports we've heard about in Rome!" "Anyway," said the elder, picking up his pace, "I'm more interested in merchandise and the world trade of ideas. Let's go see what exotic items have arrived from the East along with the religions they always bring on the trade routes. I can't wait to tell them that my God made their gods. That's my favorite sport!"

22
WICKED WORKSHOP
OF THE AIR

CRIBES! Get ready to record a new chapter of
The Lucifer Diaries so we can send it into one
of our chosen channels at the appointed time!"
FWUMP, FWUMP, FWUMP...was the noise sounding
loudly over his devilish demands as Satan flapped his bat-
style dragon wings having morphed again into that shining
serpentine reptile renowned since his entrance in Eden.
Summoning his cosmic archon Prince of Greece, his face
contorted into a mask worthy of Greek Drama. "Why is that
pesky Paul preparing to cross MY Aegean Sea...the Goat
Sea? Doesn't he know that I, as a faun Pan, the pipe-playing
goat Satyr, romp through and rule Greece as my game preserve? (Olympic Games above all!)

First having extracted a firm promise from the father of lies that he might manifest as any god he chose...Zeus... Apollo...Hermes...at the next Bacchanalia, the archon prince presented his sneering spy report: "Having done damage in Macedonia, and some verbal acrobatics in Athens, Paul is headed to Corinth."

Then barely concealing a creepy mockery for his master, the prince of Greece flew swiftly away toward the top of Mount Olympus. As a patron of the arts he felt being a goat god was beneath his dignity. Although they all were fallen angels, he suspected some were more fallen than others. And the depths dreamed up by you-know-who were the most vile ever imagined!

Meanwhile, Satan was salivating at Paul's choice of Corinth. "Gooooood! Is not Corinth my showcase city where tolerance of so-called sin became celebration of it? Just for Paul, I'll position my prostitutes like ripe fruits for plucking! Doesn't everyone in the Empire already know that 'Corinthian Girl' is the code word for prostitute? Even Paul may occasionally feel human; but why would he want to mingle with these misfits anyways? He's wasting his message on these moron mortals who never even get around to thinking about their eternal destiny...until I get them as rejects by default!"

What was that loud swooshing noise just now causing all horned heads to turn? Ominously swooping into the lineup of Dragon-angels, the Archon prince of Persia had finally arrived. Covered completely in polished black battle gear, he swore something about wanting to wait until that insufferable snob prince of Greece disappeared. Uttering a blast of expletives about his workshop being interrupted, Satan returned to reviewing his rule book.

Stroking his onyx beard, which had been chiseled to a dagger-like point, he started jabbing the air with the matching fingertip claws of his other hand. "Rule number one, and never forget it, is the more bold and big a lie, the more Earth dwellers will believe it, but only by incessant repetition! So NEVER GIVE UP!!!" Cheers went up from all the denizens of darkness for the supreme subterfuge of their Grand Master!

Taking devilish delight in this praise, his pride swelled as he continued; "We all know the endless capacity of humans to deceive themselves. This is why most of them feel more comfortable with my gleaming white persona of Lucifer the Angel of Light! Why wouldn't they believe my doctrines of denial from such an alluring appearance? It's easy to blind their minds and make unwitting captives of mortals who are ignorant of my devices.[128]

"Now moving right along from the Big Lie, we come to the veiled truth of rule number two. To wit: Truth is too stark and shocking so always dance around the truth with seven veils, beguiling them but never removing the seventh! In this regard, two taboo topics come to mind: Sin and Son! For some crazy reason, Yahweh is obsessed with sin and even takes it Personally! As I understand it, that's because He claims to have sent His Son as a bloody sacrifice to pay the people's penalty for it. So our job assignment is to insist that sin is an illusion…that there's no penalty, and all those ordinary, garden variety human mistakes don't need a savior to rescue them from. Apropos of this, there is never any Hell and a good God always finds a way to let everyone into heaven–except maybe the most extremely wicked, and us, of course who will await these dupes falling down, surprised, into our clutches!"

What was that jumping around now down at his dragon-clawed feet? Bending over to swat whatever it was, Satan saw his cute little devils trying to shout something up within earshot. Gnomes, ogres, trolls, fairies, pixies, leprechauns, and the ubiquitous entertainer elves, were all jumping and clamoring and asking in their shrill, mocking voices; "What about the Son? What about The Son? What about THE SON???"

Puffing himself up to full Dragon Divinity, Satan kicked them away with a display of smoke breathing fire and fury. "Stop that commotion or I'll excommunicate you all! When am I ever going to get respect for my great strategizing skills? That terrible tangled trinity of Father, Son and Spirit must now be turned into a travesty. It's really so devilishly easy! WE'll simply give the noxious Nazarene multiple makeovers as anything under the sun…EXCEPT The Son."

Warming to his vicious vision, the old dragon now began counting creative clones on his claws. "First and foremost will be the Jewish twist. Yeshua will be the Messiah only as a revered Rabbi or heroic healer, but NOT, (heaven forbid), the SON of G-D! If they ever believed that, they might want to invent a new holiday like those miserable Maccabees invented–Hanukkah! Then the whole world would end up singing silly songs celebrating the Earth birth of The Son to a virgin no less." Hearing that, the entertainer elves couldn't resist squealing, "Well, if they ever try that, we'll have the knowhow to subvert and mess it up!" Proud of such passionate dedication to the cause, Lucifer scooped them up as they gleefully giggled for a gliding ride on his dragon wings.

"Now back to business! No more fun and games!" snarled Satan, suddenly evicting the elevated elves. "Secondly," he continued, "for our occultists, we can create the chameleon cosmic Christ whom they can mix, match and merge with all gods in all religions. Just call it 'finding common ground for tolerance teaching.' Above all, Jesus was only a good moral example and Holy Man, with the miracles being problematic."

Winding down his workshop, the old Serpent snickered at his next bit of antiquated advice; "Don't forget to use the old story of God as an elephant surrounded by blind people feeling its different parts and each thinking they're describing Him. Naturally it will never occur to them that since Jesus claims to be the Creator of all creatures, that makes the elephant irrelevant!"

"Wait a minute!" called out a voice from the chimera hybrid beast battalion. Haven't we already got some nations worshipping elephant gods? And with your radical reincarnation idea, some of them may want to come back as elephants in their next life!" "Well said, my beastly beauties," the eternal Enemy enthused. "The more we can emphasize to these Earthlings that they're only accidental animals (and cannibals) the more they'll advance our agenda! Three cheers for Muddled Morose Mayhem and Mega-Death!!!"

Finally, their Infernal Master's monologue was getting too monotonous for his menacing masses who had heard it a million times before anyway. After reciting and reviewing every rusty rant, the ritual workshop windup had come. Resounding in space, the megaphone mouth of the Dragon rasped; "Remember the drill – NO SIN: NO SON: NO SIN: NO SON!!! All together now, practice your mantras–Good is evil and Evil is good! Our monsters are fun and Christians are the real monsters! Our gods rule and their God is dead!!!" Echoing their Elusive Eminence, his dragon angels clapped their claws, giving him a flying ovation.[129]

23

IS GOD BETTER THAN SEX?

Sea breezes blew the gathered and draped dresses against the sun-ripened shapes of the Corinthian girls causing a seductive cling. Glancing up at the great mountain behind the city, they imagined what the huge temple of the sex goddess Aphrodite looked like before the Romans destroyed it long ago. All agreed to feeling a strange affinity with their ancestors who had served as part of her rumored 1,000 male and female cult prostitutes who were considered priests and priestesses.

While preparing to ply their trade, the girls passed Poseidon's temple ("ruler of the sea"), yet the 700 year old enormous temple of Apollo was in ruins and he was missing. Now approaching the monumental gateway to the marketplace of Corinth, the girls gossiped about some of the wealthy merchants and powerful officials they had enticed the night before. At the idol temple feasts it was easy. There, in the most exciting place in town, everyone enjoyed the atmosphere. Always, the best food was served in open air restaurants, with the wildest music and lots of wine for libations, toasts and celebrations invoking the gods.

They chattered on about the festive sacrificial slain beasts and bread loaves in canisters, boiled entrails and wine in bowls. All at once, one of the girls began acting strangely, as if trying to pull them in a different direction. Out of the blue, she said, "Have you heard about these new Jews?" "Who hasn't," laughed another. "We heard they've been stirring up riots all over the empire and are accused of turning the world upside down!" "Well, weren't they proclaiming a mysterious kingdom with a king other than Caesar? No wonder they're in trouble," mocked a third girl.[130]

Finally, begging them all to stop and sit on a bench near the bakery, the first girl was clearly trying to control some new emotions. Smelling the addictive aroma of fresh baked bread, they didn't notice the noise of grain grinding, pounding, kneading, and the crackle of fire from the ovens. As everywhere in the Empire, they were grateful for the golden wheat from Egypt and their invention of bolting to make the flour fine and white. Atavistic appetites were stirring in their souls for this universally acclaimed "staff of life."

Determined to be heard, their friend leaned over close and began speaking hurriedly in a heavy whisper, "I have to confess I slipped away from the idol feast last night to search for the synagogue. A crowd was listening outside the windows of the house next door, and I also tried to hear what the message was. Just then, a lovely lady named Priscilla came out and befriended me. Her voice was so soothing and her eyes were like pools of peace, which I had never seen before![131]

"As we sat in a serene garden, gilded by a full moon, she began telling me about this fantastic God who came to the Earth He had created by being born as a baby to a virgin. He lived a perfect life to offer Himself as a sacrifice for the sins of the world because of His great love for us, His creatures." As her friends were raising their eyebrows and clapping their hands over their mouths, one of them, smirking, demanded "And just where is this God-Man now? We know what the Romans do with crucified criminals!"

Expressing exasperation with folded arms and tossed back hair, their companion took a deep breath and continued: "Last night was what the Jews call Erev Shabbat, the beginning of their one day off from work out of every seven. Can you believe that the Empire allows it? They say their God created everything in six days and rested on the seventh, giving it to them as a holy day to remember Him. But please come with me tonight to the meeting of those called Christianoi (Partisans of Messiah) to celebrate His rising from the dead on the first day."[132]

As darkness descended and the welcome coolness came, the group split up, with some slinking off to the snake god sanctuary (Asklepios), seeking their salary of seduction. Then to those who were left, lingering in suspense, she spread out her hands in hope saying, "Last night, there was a great power in the words spoken that pierced my heart drawing me to some unknown, overwhelming love. I couldn't wait to tell you today! I really want you to meet Priscilla. She's like the dream mother you never had! Can you hear the singing now? Isn't it other-worldly and heavenly?" To their protests of immodest dress while now nearing the assembly house, she loosed some lumps under her skirts, laughingly saying; "Don't worry, here are some shawls to cover your heads and shoulders. Now you look holy–except for all the makeup!"

Pressing through the crowd at the open doorway, they were shocked to see all sorts of people sitting together who would never be found in the same room! Gathered were slaves, nobles, merchants, students, philosophers, sailors, butchers, bakers, rabbis, scribes, men, women, children of all ages and races and even the ruler of the synagogue and Roman soldiers. After looking around and recognizing some local thieves, drunkards, adulterers and sodomites, they relaxed and felt more comfortable than expected. "Actually, we fit right in this strange spectacle, don't we?" said one as they elbowed each other with a giggle.[133]

Squeezing around the groups at tables, Priscilla waved as she caught their eyes. Leading them out to a corner of the courtyard under a canopy of stars, she sat the girls down on cushions in a circle, with herself at the center. Then, flashing a smile at each face, Priscilla said a silly thing. "Want to become again like a child and enter an invisible kingdom which even overrules the Roman Empire? You know what? We are the real royals! God is a romantic. He wants to capture your heart forever, for private, exclusive passionate devotion. No rival gods. He's jealous and zealous for your soul because he poured out His blood to make you a super immortal!"

The perplexed prostitutes were mute, carried away far beyond their comprehension. Priscilla continued; "All these people that you see are not what they used to be. At the cross, class distinctions dissolved!" As skeptical looks lined their brows, one girl blurted out what she knew they were all wondering; "Why would a complete stranger, from far away in another country, care enough to die for us?" Extending her arms and hands out to them all in a huge welcome gesture, Priscilla explained; "Because He created you and everything else for His pleasure and wants to collect a cosmic forever family to share it all with.

"Do you know why He always wants the good news of His kingdom to be given to the most sinful people? Because those who are forgiven more, love more! He even said that the hairs on your head are all numbered Imagine! When you ran your comb through them today, number 15,825 and number 40,556 may have fallen out, but they will grow right back." At this, all the girls were pulling their fingers through their hair with happy, hilarious laughter!"[134]

But now, what were those other sounds suddenly erupting? Wild weeping was breaking through as one of the girls flung herself at the feet of her new friend. "Many men have said they loved me, but I know none of them would have died for me. I feel so filthy. I want to come to the cross to be cleansed by Jesus!" Priscilla, sobbing, hugging and rocking her like a long lost motherless child, laid hands on her head in prayer: "Welcome Home my new daughter and sister to the Kingdom of Glory which has been awaiting your arrival. Do you know the angels are now having a celebration just for you?"

Wiping away tears of joy still streaming down her face, the new convert cried out; "I'll need to change my friends and flee my former way of life and learn how to work. Please, please Priscilla, can I stay with you and learn about this holy living and hear the messages Jesus spoke? Teach me how to grow into my new self. How can the Holy Spirit be my guide?" Patting her head with a calming caress, Priscilla held out a new white dress. "Yes, yes, this is for your baptism and I'd love for you to stay! We're now family forever!"

One day, about one week later, the girl was wondering if it might be time to venture out of her wonderful spiritual cocoon for the first time. Why not? Wouldn't she have to confront her old world out there sometime? She knew her faith would be tested from now on, but felt confident of victory. Feeling the comfort and companionship of the Holy Spirit strong inside her, she spoke and sang mysteries back to Him in the thrilling angel language He had blessed her with. But then it happened![135]

Unexpectedly, a sudden surge of sympathy suffused her spirit and she ran wildly toward a temple of pagan sacrifice. At the meat market next to it, she pulled at the pigs, sheep and goats about to be slaughtered, screaming, "Don't you know you don't have to offer the blood of animals to placate the gods? The Son of God has sacrificed Himself once and for all!" Dragging away the distraught daughter of the goddess, as they supposed her to still be, the butcher and pagan priest scratched their heads asking, "Whatever has possessed this prostitute now?"[136]

Seeing her slumped in the square sobbing, a sailor stopped to soothe her and seek some sex. Lifting her head in his rope-rough hands, he was surprised by her eyes. Instead of the familiar decadent dullness, they were vibrantly glowing with new life! "What happened to you?" he said, staring. "Oh, I tried to save some sacrifices," she stammered. "No, I mean your eyes, you've changed!" "Yes, have I ever!" she exclaimed. "Instead of a prostitute, I'm a princess! Now my Father is the King of Kings instead of Satan the father of lies."

Quickly seizing the moment, she continued; "I know you're bewildered, but would you be willing to be a witness to miracles? Paul, an ambassador of Messiah, is praying today for the sick, casting out demons and laying on hands for the baptism in the Holy Spirit. You'll see signs and wonders!" As she swiftly picked herself up and ran off for the five hour daily siesta time, he began slowly following, unable to fathom who she had become.

Now the high heat of the sun had begun shimmering and glistening in the crystal clear Grecian air. Passing by what turned out to be the house of Stephanas, strange singing sounds were entering his ears, like long lost lovely languages from other stars or planets. What was this otherworldly harmony? Just then appearing as if out of nowhere, a man in a Roman toga quickly walked up bedside him saying, "Doesn't it sound out of this world? Please come in and meet some citizens of a kingdom that is not of this world. It's far beyond the rare, coveted privilege of Roman citizenship, I assure you!"

Finding the suspense irresistible, the sailor accepted the stranger's invitation...while also smelling the scent of the simmering midday meals he knew were now being served everywhere in the city. Joining all types and classes of other men, young and old, he reclined on one of the couches ringed around the triclinium table. His host, named Aquila, began speaking as bunches of grapes, plates of cheese, olives, and bread appeared. Next came a salad of fresh herbs and warm bowls of egg and lemon chicken broth in which the long egg-laying career of an old hen had deliciously ended. Then followed bowls of stewed vegetables and a variety of dried fruits, along with glasses of water to which some wine was added for purification.

Aquila and the other Jewish believers pronounced the ritual blessings in Hebrew, while the others agreed in Greek. Calling the cooks and servers in to thank them profusely, Aquila said; "Coming from Rome, I always enjoy your traditional Greek chicken soup, especially with a hint of mint. Speaking of Rome, have you all heard why my wife, Priscilla and I were expelled from the city along with all the other Jews? It was because Claudius Caesar was alarmed that the controversy over Christ was causing riots! But God used the opportunity to lead us here to Corinth and connect us with Paul for a most fruitful mission."

Distracted by some muffled mockery erupting among a group of students, Aquila stopped and challenged them to an open debate. Accepting the offer, one young man blurted out; "What is this hilarious 'Harpazo' we're hearing about?" "Imagine," he scoffed, "an old widowed grandma, obscure and unknown, rises from the grave as a lovely young woman and rules the world! Millions of others, dead or alive, rise out of prisons, oceans, shipwrecks, even eaten by cannibals....all being grabbed up by Jesus in the clouds to later take over Earth as the NEW immortals! Isn't this the craziest fantasy ever? A lot of us Greeks think the idea of raising up dead bodies is pretty gruesome."

Standing up to get all the slumbering diners' attention, Aquila raised his arm and loudly announced; "Regarding this young man's comments, let's have a vote now on two possible choices God could offer us! Number One: As your popular Stoic philosophers teach: We all die and merge with nature as disembodied spirits in the cosmos; OR Number Two; A loving God renovates Earth and nature back to something like His original creation of Eden. Also He gives those who love Him fabulous supernatural bodies to enjoy ruling it with His Son, the King who conquered death forever.

"This is the new creation nation now being formed to inherit the world to come; what our Hebrew prophets call the 'Olam HaBa.' Since we are to be the extended Body of Messiah, our bodies will glow like His; walk through walls and locked doors like His; appear and disappear like His; and pass through the heavens from Earth and back like His! This is the choice Jesus died to offer you. But if you're unable to believe that HE Himself came back from the dead and is now alive, then you can't have His promise of hope for this future. And by the way, He cannot lie.

"Remember, our God made your gods for which your Greek word is demons! Jesus said 'Salvation is from the Jews.' So why not join Paul and me and his other companions as we travel through the empire planting kingdom colonies of Olam HaBa (the age to come)![137]

24
THE LOVE TO DIE FOR

L ike fish flopping out of water, ships were rumbling on rollers between the two ports of Corinth, separated by a narrow isthmus.

Who was the woman walking toward the western wharf to embark on a ship headed for Rome? No one knew she carried a secret document destined to change the world! But Phoebe was fearless as she fingered the scroll secured safely in her sash. Since the simplest writing materials were extremely expensive, and the public mail system of the empire was very slow, Paul never sent his letters by Roman post office. As ambassador of Messiah, King of the cosmos, he only trusted kingdom-minded couriers with what would be New Covenant scriptures.

Knowing Phoebe would need a travelling companion, Priscilla had recently brought over her ex-prostitute convert, saying, "why not bless her with a dress and make her your protégé?" Having burned up her sexy streetwalker garments of sheer, nearly see-through materials, the girl was wearing just a simple, humble tunic from her baptism. Being a patroness of Paul and in a position to help many others, Phoebe had the means to outfit her for the 800 mile trip to Rome. Asking if she was ready to learn to read and write and memorize the oracles of God, they had both hugged like a new mother and daughter as Phoebe counseled her on clothing. "Now you'll need some modest but regal styles and especially fabrics that will flow in the angelic ring dances at our Agape feasts."

Then flashing a big smile with a little laugh toward her new young friend, Phoebe added, "Now remember, just natural hair styles and a minimum of jewelry, because you've changed from a woman of the streets to a woman of God! Did you know that King David even wrote a prophecy about us in his Psalms? 'The Lord gave the command; the women who proclaim the good news are a great army.'"[138]

Finally reaching Rome, the two weary women were overwhelmed at the sight. Claiming to be the center of the world, this great city of millions mingled opulence and squalor. Great blocks of tall buildings rose high over narrow, congested streets crowded with multitudes, both slave and free from many tribes and nations. Most lived in fear of fire and the constant noise of carts kept them awake at night.

But despite their great luxury, even emperors and nobles also lived in fear.

Beyond the inner city, toward the pinnacle of the Emperor's palace on Capitolene Hill, were stately white marble villas and great colonnaded forums for business, trade and talk. But city tours could wait. Right now it was Saturday evening, and Phoebe knew hundreds of house groups were meeting to celebrate the Divine Lover of their souls. Entering the door of a typical Roman home and being welcomed by the host, the two "sisters" were elated at the sights and sounds of the Agape (Love Feast) in progress across the large open courtyard. With the flutes, harps, tambourines, singing, dancing and clapping, it seemed like a party in paradise!

Imitating the ring dances of the angels gave them a sacred sample of heaven on Earth. Spontaneous participation of worship, prophecies, praise, scripture readings and healings progressed as the presence of God began to be felt. Later, as the food was brought out, Phoebe and her friend found their seats and prepared for communion. After one of the leaders stood up and blessed the cup and the bread, it was all passed around from person to person to remember the Lord's death until He returns. As they ate, the believers discussed the things of God, quoting the scriptures from memory by necessity since very few could obtain even one book of the Bible.

Then Phoebe, feeling it was time to present her prize, positioned herself next to a teacher. Holding out the scroll, she introduced herself as a minister of the assembly in

Cenchrea near Corinth. "Paul the Apostle commissioned me to carry his precious document to the whole congregation in Rome. So now you'll need to rent a large facility to gather all the city house groups together for its public reading." After hearing the announcement, a sense of awe began to spread and all were in suspense because of this special letter and what profound teachings might be revealed in it.

In the first century Roman Empire, spirituality was diverse. Tolerance was nearly total, as long as the emperor and state were given supreme loyalty. Philosophy and new eastern religions had eclipsed the old gods. The Egyptian goddess Isis had many priests and an impressive ritual and the Persian god Mithras had great appeal to soldiers. Many who were near despair worshipped chance, luck, astrology and magic.

But a very odd, new message of outrageous love was making inroads, even in Caesar's household. It seemed they talked about a heavenly kingdom with a God-King who actually loved Earth people. This God was even supposed to be the Creator of the universe and yet loved the world so much He came incognito as a Man to die for everybody's sins, even on a Roman cross! So if God had become a Human to offer His Blood to make humans immortal, then all "immortals" philosophies and religions were beside the point.

What was the official reaction to Him? Just as Jesus had predicted, they hated both Him and His followers. They were denounced as a "strange and illegal superstition," suspected and accused of the worst crimes; namely atheism for rejecting all so-called "gods," and especially the Emperor himself being worshipped as a god! Also "brothers and sisters" having secret rituals of eating bread as the "Body" of their God was alarming. They were said to hate all other people and were making the gods so angry that all weather calamities and natural disasters were blamed on them!

Then why was their number growing by leaps and bounds into an "immense multitude?" Because the supernatural power of the Holy Spirit was changing and liberating them like nothing else could. Bodies and minds were healed. Depression and demons disappeared. Hopelessness dissolved into happiness. Deep peace and joy remained in all circumstances, no matter what. But hope for a fantastic, unfathomable future was what made Messiah the Love to die for!

The next month on a moonlit night, Phoebe's protégé and companion carefully headed toward the trash dump. "Let's recite Psalm 91 and pray for protection by the angels as we walk," said one and they both agreed, quietly using their supernatural Spirit languages. Each was hugging a Hebrew prayer shawl, folded under their arms to use as a tiny tent for the treasure they were out to hunt.

"The stench is getting more intense so it can't be far," they nodded while beginning to cough. Linking arms they prayed, "Lord Jesus, please sharpen our ears to hear the cries and speed our feet to run fast and make us invisible, Amen." Both began to climb around the heaps, holding their noses and listening intently. When muffled moans of newborn babies were detected, they each dived into the debris to rescue a tiny sacred soul.

Cautiously dripping some jugs of donated mother's milk into their mouths, they blessed and bundled up each infant in the Tallits and ran rejoicing. Breathlessly beating on the door of the designated house, when it opened, the mother with much milk made ready to feed them both, while others went for water to clean them up. Then the whole family laughed and sang and praised God, shouting to the sisters in the Lord, "Congratulations on your first Baby Run! HalleluYah!"

"If you'll excuse us now," said the two smugglers, "we'd like to go find Priscilla and Aquila's house. We can't wait to tell them all about it! Isn't it a blessing that they could move back to Rome, since Emperor Claudius died? Did you know they made these prayer shawls with Paul? In Corinth, they teamed up in the same trade making Tallit 'tents' with all these knots, tassels and fringes to remind us of God's laws, as well as the blue cords on the corners. I'm sure you all remember how everybody who touched these on the edge of Yeshua's shawl was healed!"[139]

Then moving to the door with hugs and goodbyes, the two girls turned to remind the family "We'll be back soon to find out what you've named these babies and don't forget to tuck them in the tallits to hurry their healing!"

Back at Aquila and Priscilla's house, they were introduced to a very brave and courageous girl. Being from nobility, she had to defy cultural and religious traditions of the family and friends to pursue her own destiny, as revealed by the Living God. Having heard the scripture story of Gideon, she had gone home and smashed some of the household idol-replicas of the city gods. Needless to say, she lost everything and was expelled from her house and disinherited. She said, "It was a small price to pay for the peace and joy Jesus has given me, and I was blessed to escape with my life and be rescued by Priscilla." Reaching out to take her hand in both her own, the Corinthian girl looked into her eyes with tears saying, "How well I know, she actually rescued me too!"[140]

This aristocratic girl had indeed been given divine protection. Roman fathers ruled by whim with absolute power of life and death over their children. The babies they didn't want, they drowned or threw out on the trash heap. In anger, they could whip and beat their children and divorce their wives for trivial reasons. It was the custom to treat their mistresses better than their wives. But why not? The Emperor himself, Nero Caesar, specialized in pomposities and atrocities. However, nobody knew how unbelievably bad it was about to get.

But meanwhile, for over twelve years, the good news and power of the Kingdom to come had been spreading like wildfire to the farthest parts of the empire. Jesus' twelve apostles were unstoppable, proclaiming His message with miracles to prove it in Persia, Babylon, India, Armenia, Egypt, Spain, Ethiopia, Sudan, North Africa and beyond! Soon however, back in Rome, another kind of fire was about to be kindled, leading to insatiable innovations in the evil entertainments of terror. The victims' only "crime" would be as nonconformists to a depraved society. By opting out of what their God had forbidden, they were accused of hating the human race even though they were always doing acts of love and charity.

Surfeited, saturated and intoxicated after one of his most lavish feasts, the young Caesar Nero stretched out his body on an opulent bed. As familiar spirits began to speak in his mind, he sometimes wondered where these thoughts were coming from. But they had always been so much a part of his life he just assumed they were his own ideas or perhaps a "muse" given to him by the gods.

"You're not appreciated enough for your great talents," they said. "You need to schedule longer command performances for your superb theatrical singing. Just because the length of your last concert caused people to fall asleep and a woman to even give birth, doesn't mean they weren't impressed with your voice. You'll have to agree that the 100 foot statue of yourself in the huge entrance hall surpasses all previous Emperors not to mention the gold, jewels and pearl everywhere in you palace."

Nero nodded knowingly as he joined the conversation with his invisible friends. "Don't forget my dining rooms with ivory ceilings and rotating panels that rain down flowers with concealed sprinklers to shower my guests with perfume," he exclaimed in awesome delight. "Yes," replied the unseen entities. "But we're most impressed by your circular main banquet hall with the revolving dome rotating day and night to mirror the heavens!" "Of course," the Emperor enthused, "Everyone should be astounded because I had to bring in convicts from all over the empire to work on these fabulous projects."

Suddenly a strange silence settled in his skull. Why had his cosmic mentors stopped voicing their agreement? But just then sad, depressing moaning sounds emanated from the ethereal advisors. "Sorry," they sniffed, "but we just can't help feeling disgusted with the shoddy surrounding city as an unworthy setting for the magnificence of the glory of your unprecedented palace. Suppose you were to find a way to totally renovate and rebuild Rome on a grandiose scale and rename the city after yourself?"

Imagine! A conflagration great enough to light up the night sky for a week of blazing beauty! Fire would take on a whole new history with the name of Nero. Overwhelmed by this stupendous vision, a hypnotic sleep seized him and a diabolical dream descended into his head. Then it startled him awake and sitting up suddenly, he exclaimed, "My spirit guides have just given me the most dramatic scenario ever. A sort of sample or rehearsal of this fabulous fire! I'll invite the elite to a gorgeous garden party illuminated by human torches! Wax soaked shirts can be put on Christians and then when we crucify them on high stakes all around the pavilions, they can be set ablaze to burn brightly and light up all the festivities!" Hearing his gleeful laughing echoing down the palace halls, the many Christians in Caesar's household service were unaware of the source of its inspiration.

But Rome had sold its soul for entertainment. The Circus Maximus, an ancient chariot racing stadium, had been the setting for triumphal processions, flamboyant parades, public games, religious festivals, Gladiators, beast hunts, dancers and musicians. A dusty space with shops and booths, it was a colorful, crowded, disreputable area frequented by prostitutes, jugglers, fortune tellers and low-class performing artists. But now, human blood sacrifice was about to become the new favorite spectator sport. In the massive arena, 150,000 could clamor for an Olympics of Blood. Paved with sand to absorb the red liquid life of its victims, it would be unique in the technology of torture. Free food went along with the fun and the government provided bread to the fans in the stands. Rome was known for "Fiat Panis" (Let there be bread), meaning "Bread and Circuses!"

The year was 64 A.D. and on a hot summer night, fires flared everywhere. Massive columns of orange flames erupting in black stinking smoke were unstoppable. Frantically pushing and praying their way through the screaming mobs, the two baby run friends had to get to the house to rescue the now young children. The roaring fire had not yet reached their family, so everyone thankfully plunged their Tallits in a water barrel, wrapped them around their heads and arms and ran for the open fields. Over the cries of the panicked crowds of refugees, they could be heard loudly proclaiming the promises of Psalm 91.

Yet after a whole week of thousands dying while three-fourths of the city burned, nearly everyone knew that Nero had done it and even that he had admired its beauty while reciting the fall of Troy! But there was only one group hated enough on which he could successfully place the blame. The surviving followers of the Lamb of God would become the scapegoats. Though many had escaped the fire, their real ordeal had just begun. But why did the test of their faithfulness have to be so extreme? Because the promised rewards were far more eternally extreme!

Falsely accused, though innocent of any crimes, vast throngs of Jesus lovers were being arrested, quickly "tried" and condemned. Trapped among these masses being herded toward the Arena, the two baby run friends suddenly spotted their new aristocratic acquaintance. Yelling her name and pushing through to hug her, all three vowed to die together. But as they were nearing the entrance to the Circus Maximus, one of the champion Gladiators swiftly pulled them aside from the bloodthirsty roars of the crowd and beasts, leading the three fugitives down into a secretive underground chamber.

Speaking respectfully to the brave social outcast, he said in a hushed tone of bewilderment; "I recognized you as being from one of our most famous noble families, usually seated in a prominent position near the Emperor! What are you doing here? Don't you know what they are going to do to all of you? You'll be sewed up in the skins of wild beasts to be bitten to death by dogs or you'll be tied to the horns of a bull to be murdered on a re-enactment of the myth of Dirce. Or be dismembered by animals or set on fire as living torches!"

Hearing his horrible words sent a shudder through her body, squeezing out inadvertent tears. But taking a deep breath and tightly linking arms with her two companions, she boldly stared him in the eyes saying, "I have counted the cost and it's nothing compared to the reward! My Lord Yeshua said that if we don't love Him more than our family members and our own life, then we are not worthy of Him." "Not only that," added one of her friends, "But his radical rules require us to love our enemies, bless those who curse us, do good to those who hate us, pray for those who despitefully use us, and jump for joy when we're persecuted because great is our reward in heaven." "Amen!" agreed the other two, "not to mention we have to forgive everybody or God won't forgive us, because Jesus asked forgiveness for those who had just nailed Him to a cross! So if the Son of God forgave His torturers, who are we not to forgive Nero? Are we better than God?"[141]

Shaking his head at what sounded to him like insanity, the Gladiator exclaimed, "Now I know why that huge collection of Christian convicts out there is singing hymns so loudly that nobody can even hear the lions roar. You people all have to be crazy!" Feeling a spiritual chill from the kingdom of darkness, the three began to recoil at the suffocating subterranean vault of slimy, dark stones. This brutal man whose manner might turn menacing was full of scars and wounds around the sweaty, heavy leather holding his muscled body. Choking back a cough and in a surge of compassion, one of the Christ-followers asked, "Please tell us what your life has been like?"

Resisting the urge for sarcasm, and slumping sideways, he averted his eyes from their curiosity. "At the Gladiator training school I lived like the rest of the criminals, slaves and prisoners of war in a barracks cell barely big enough to turn around in. During the day, we each desperately hacked away at a thick wooden post as a mock enemy. We knew we would sweat and bleed until we died, but still we hoped for a few brief moments of glory. Our rewards for those brutal days were baths with hot, cold and lukewarm water, and hearty plentiful meals of meat, grains and cereals. We had tiny sleeping cells but a large training hall with heated floors. We had a very small chance for survival, fame and possibly liberty. If we could advance to top status, the ultimate goal was to attain freedom."

Moved by his story, the ex-Corinthian girl said, "Jesus set me free from the bondage of prostitution." Then the ex-socialite said, "And Jesus set me free from the arrogance of privilege." But the third young woman was more to the point; "Even if against all odds you win your freedom; then what? It won't last forever after you die! Only if you know

His truth will Jesus set you eternally free from hell which is infinitely more tortuous than anything in your life!"[142]

The Gladiator gaped with incredulity at such a scary supernatural scenario. "No!" he protested. "I believe like the Epicurean philosophers that the world has come about by the chance meeting of atoms. I'll just dissolve into the cosmos and cease to exist!" Visibly upset, the three friends now felt frantic for his salvation. "Impossible!" they all exclaimed. "Your real self, spirit and soul, live forever in either heaven or hell! At death, you just leave your body like a person going out of their house. If you go to one of the dwellings Jesus has been preparing for us in heaven, you will have bliss and ecstasy! As the Psalmist said 'In His presence is fullness of joy; At His right hand are pleasures forevermore.'"[143]

"Are you three trying to allure me with these fantasies?" groaned the Gladiator, putting his rough, scarred hands over his ears. "I'm tired of listening to you! Now I know you're some kind of alien and you weren't joking when you said you were not of this world." "That's right!" they all laughed, lifting up their hands. "It is written that our citizenship is in heaven, but don't forget, the Kingdom of Heaven is going to come down here on Earth! It will be an invasion of the NEW immortals (that's us), evicting the old immortals, whom you call your gods."[144]

Finally reaching the end of his endurance with being confused by this conversation, the Gladiator grabbed hold of the girls' hands to lead them back up to the ferocious beasts (both man and animal). As he reluctantly led them through the precarious passage, the three thanked him for his kindness to them. Now out again in the searing sunlight, the noises and smells emanating from this theatre of torture threatened to overwhelm them. Only by speaking the words of God hidden in their hearts, could they feel peace as hate moved in for the kill. But before saying goodbye to the Gladiator, they couldn't resist giving him one final glimpse of the future.

Pointing toward the arena and visibly moved with pity, the ex-prostitute asked, "Haven't you ever felt sorry for these tragic, tormented beasts, caged and starved to force vicious attacks? They too are groaning to be liberated from the bondage of suffering!" Knowing this captive audience couldn't last, the aristocrat carefully explained, "Our teacher, Apostle Paul wrote a letter to us at Rome saying that the whole cosmos and all its creatures are waiting for the children of God to appear and bring liberty from corruption. That's because when God's kingdom comes ("Olam Haba"), nature will be restored to its original creation condition like in Eden.[145]

"Before parting, may my friends and I paint the word picture God gave to Isaiah the prophet depicting His plan for this planet?" Thinking that they were just stalling for time, the Gladiator gave in. So with faces radiant, the trio raised their voices and recited:

"The wolf also shall dwell with the lamb,
the leopard shall lie down with the young
goat, the calf and the young lion and the
fatling together, and a little child shall lead
them. The lion shall eat straw like the ox, the
nursing child shall play by the Cobra's hole,
the weaned child shall put his hand in the
viper's den. They shall not hurt nor destroy
in all My holy mountain. For the Earth shall
be full of the knowledge of the Lord as the
waters cover the sea."[146]

Transfixed and astonished, the Gladiator gasped, "Does
your God always proclaim the impossible?" "Of course,"
they laughed, "because He's the only One who can do it!
Shalom, goodbye for now. We'll be praying for you to see
you again in the kingdom to come." Then the Gladiator
gruffly rebuffed their gesture to lay hands on his head for a
blessing, saying; "All right, enough! Go! Run and join your
comrades."

Sad that they must experience the slaughter to which
he was long accustomed, a heart gripping emotion began
to enter his being. Everything they had said was resonating
and whirling in his mind. Watching them walk toward the
massive mob of martyrs, whom they had insisted were all
their brothers and sisters in a supernatural family, his soul
suddenly split with a jolt of jealousy. Then the sun-bronzed

creased leather of his face felt the first tear coolly dripping down it in more years then he could remember. Maybe he would try a prayer after all or else those three shining faces would haunt him! What could he lose since he had to risk his life everyday anyway?

His sacrificial scapegoat acquaintances were already pouring out of their hearts in high praises of worship, continuing to blot out the roars of the lions, whose teeth would tear into their flesh. They boldly refused to surrender their souls, which would soon soar up to their Savior. Later, when his turn came to battle the beasts, the gladiator entered the arena and groaned when he saw their three naked bodies totally covered in blood along with many others, as the spectators shouted, "Well washed!"

Life was cheap in the empire, but this was a different dimension. A righteous rage rose up inside him and he vowed to avenge his three otherworldly friends by fighting as never before to win his freedom!

25
TEMPLE TERROR

Reminiscing by the river, Lydia lingered in a dreamy meditation. In her mind's eye, scenes would fly from that first life-changing encounter at this very same spot. There was Paul, with his small intense eyes under furrowed brows in a thin face tapering toward a dark pointed beard. Approaching her with his companions, he knew that she and her group of women were worshipping the Living God because of the Jewish custom of meeting by flowing water on the Sabbath when a city had no synagogue. Likewise, Lydia knew these men were Jews by their tallit prayer shawls. So when they sat down and began boldly proclaiming Yeshua the Messiah being crucified and rising from the dead, she still could feel the chill and thrill of this news! God had opened her heart to believe His Son was waiting to return from heaven and she and her whole household were baptized in that river right away!

Purple dye was the reason why Lydia lived in Philippi. What was that power of purple? Being highly prized by pagan priests, by royalty and the rich, it was required by kings and for other things. The more important you were as a Roman senator, the more purple decoration you had on your tunic and toga, but only the Emperor would wear a toga made entirely of purple cloth! For the embellishment of the elite, it was extracted drop by drop from millions of Murex mollusks, the tiny little shellfish which alone provided this precious purple, said to be worth its weight in silver!

Hospitality was holy and Lydia had learned the art of it early at her father's estate in Thyatira, the great purple production center of Roman Asia (modern day Turkey). There being no sons in her family, she was trained to take over the business when her father died. But the problem was becoming a merchant princess of purple tied her into the trade guilds requiring religious debauchery in the pagan tradition. Also later on, Lydia, like many other Greeks, felt drawn to the moral message heard in the Jewish synagogues. Then after becoming a worshipper of the Most High God, she finally fled to Philippi with her whole inheritance and household.

Being a Roman colony on the Rome to Asian trade route, Philippi was the perfect place to sell purple goods. Having been the birthplace of Alexander the Great, Philippi was a uniquely favored city in the empire. Was this the reason the Lord had rewarded Lydia with a lovely, large house? She assumed this divine appointment with Paul was a call to use God's provision for hospitality. So, boldly taking the initiative, she kept persistently insisting they all stay with her until they finally agreed.[147]

Later on, after Paul left with his other co-workers, Luke stayed behind in Philippi to solidify the new congregation. He was the constant companion, biographer and doctor who had not only kept Paul alive after floggings and shipwrecks, but also wrote a book with more details on the life of Jesus. Now perceiving that the most problematic topic was the resurrection, the Lord led Luke to lecture on the supernatural. Lydia's household had been blessed as the nucleus of the new assembly of Messiah in the city, which had been multiplying steadily. So many new converts were intrigued with the transformation being promised to them, that they would love to hear Luke's explanation.

When the evening arrived, an Erev Shabbat dinner was shared along with the holy communion elements, after which everyone began to listen intently as Luke stood up to teach. "Did you think Jesus rose from the dead in His same body? Certainly not! And we don't either! It was a totally new, supernatural body-type that never existed before–a super-immortal body! It glows! It goes anywhere in the universe at the speed of thought! It appears and disappears, walks through walls and locked doors, and can eat and drink for pleasure, but not by necessity to stay alive," Luke explained. "As a physician, I'm amazed at the anatomy! In our natural realm it's impossible, of course but our supernatural flesh-and-bone-only bodies won't have any organs, arteries or veins because there won't be any blood to operate them! Our divine bodies will literally be temples of the Holy Spirit, Who will fill us inside and will overflow out of us to make us glow!"

"So, we're supposed to get these glowing, bloodless bodies? It sounds frightfully ghostly!" quipped a young philosophy scholar. After that outburst, many of the youth were finding it hard to contain a chuckle, while trying to visualize their future faces. Soon, Luke had to laugh too. "Yes it does sound a bit bizarre but we will still look like real people, with all our original skin colors except we'll be shining with glory wherever we go! Also, there will be pleasures in our supernatural flesh among other things. It is written in the Psalms, 'In His presence is fullness of joy; At His right hand are pleasures forevermore.'" (Psalms 16:11)

Still mystified by much of this message, another young student, raising both hands with a shrug, asked; "But what is the purpose? Why will we need these fantastic bodies?" Immediately, Luke leveled a barrage of answers that mangled this young scholar's mindset: "To judge and rule the world and the angels, and so our enemies can't kill us anymore! It's axiomatic that immortals always rule over mortals. Remember when Satan and his fallen angels came down to corrupt the Earth with sex, violence and sorcery even creating human-animal hybrids? It took the global flood of Noah to destroy the works of these Nephilim, whom we Greeks revere as our gods and chronicle their awful exploits in our mythology."

Although some in the group were getting a bit groggy, Luke lit the oil lamps and continued on. "All these idol temples and shrines you see still around everywhere are like souvenirs of the time when they walked on the Earth. Never forget that these angels, who turned into the demon-gods, existed before time began. They even sang with joy to see Earth created, God's special masterpiece, and it's even like heaven's mirror with its menagerie. But these creatures are planning to make a come-back. Didn't Jesus say that the time of His return would be like the days of Noah BEFORE the flood? Wasn't that exactly where the giants, mighty heroes, Nephilim, Atlantis and pyra-mids originated?"

At this, the philosophy scholar sat up straight with a star-tled look, exclaiming, "Now I think I get it! We have to have these super immortal bodies ourselves to fight and destroy these ancient monsters. I just remembered how Isaiah the Prophet saw that just before the coming of the Lord. The land of Israel would be full of idols and sorcery just like in the old days!" Imagine! How could they revert that far back when, right now, in the first century, they're not doing any of that, but complaining about the Romans and Greeks putting THEIR idols in the land?"[148]

Luke applauded announcing, "You're amazingly close to the climax for which our glorious bodies are designed which will be total banishment of every so called god that ever existed.

But in the meantime, Messiah commanded us to tell His good news in all the nations, so many more can become new super immortals and rule in His kingdom! Who else could ever offer us a hope like that?"

As it was now getting late and into the first day of the week (the Sunday Resurrection Celebration), the assembly members were filing out, now feeling a formidable sense of awe at their future. While Luke was leaving, Lydia left him with a profound insight. "I remember reading that Jesus said the lake of fire was created for the devil and his angels. Now I thank you for letting us know how and when they are finally going to get there!" Turning back for a moment at the door, with a face of foreboding, Luke responded, "But by far the most shocking thing I think Jesus ever said was that He would send all those who failed to help His needy followers to the same place!" "But, on the other hand, anyone who gave even one of them a cup of cold water will receive a reward," reminded Lydia, waving goodbye.[149]

Now it was about thirteen years later, and over in the Holy Land some children were saying, "Let's play Olam Haba! You be the wolf and I'll be the lamb!" "No, your hair is a darker color than mine, so I should be the lamb." "Well, all right, this time I'll let you have your way. Here's some hay, so let's pretend we're dwelling together." "Can you imagine such a thing?

It's so funny!" Then the "wolf" stopped howling and licked the "lamb's face and both children rolled in the grass, giggling.

Now other brothers and sisters were running over to get in the game of the future peaceable kingdom, pictured by Isaiah Ha Navi. "Please let me be the leopard that lies down with the little goat," called out a larger boy, already rubbing spots on his arms with a little lump of charcoal. Then his youngest brother, picking up some ropes shouted, "And I'll be the little child who leads the calf and young lion and yearling together!"

"But what about the cow and the bear? "Who can moo and who can growl and who will be the bear's cubs and the cow's calves to lie down and graze together?" asked their mother as she carried the youngest baby over to watch. "Could you first dig a cobra hole so I can put your little sister here down to play by it? And don't forget to scoop out a viper's den so I can put your two year old cousin's hand on it."

"Oh Ima!" all the little ones sighed. "The sun's getting so hot. Now, it must be time for supper and a rest." One of the children asked, "What have you and grandmother and great grandmother been cooking today?" She replied, "I'll tell you after you finish feeding your transformed animals. Remember, the lion has to eat straw like the ox and then we'll all recite the end of the story together for today's memory lesson." Then trudging up the hill, hungry and hot, every little tot tried to sing and shout:

"They will not hurt or destroy
In all My holy mountain,
For the Earth will be full
Of the knowledge of the Lord
As the waters cover the sea." (Isaiah 11:9)

Watching her great-grandchildren from the rooftop, Rhoda remembered that unforgettable, fateful day of her own childhood. Here in Pella, their city of refuge from the revolt in Jerusalem, they were safe beyond the east bank of the Jordan River. Gazing on these hills and valleys and springs, she could see again the grass of Galilee, where so many thousands waited to hear the words of the Miracle Worker. Never had she forgotten the thrill of the blessing of the Lord Yeshua himself, gathering her and other little children up in his big, strong carpenter's arms (over the protests of His disciples) and laying his healing hands on each of their heads. From that moment on, she knew she would love Him forever, even after all these years, her spine still tingled when she thought about it!

Now needing to delay this daydreaming, her strong hands twisted the wet cloth of squeeze cheese out of the drained yogurt. After pressing pinches of sea salt and herbs into the creamy lump, Rhoda rubbed a silken sample over her tongue for approval. Then, with an olive wood paddle, she pushed it down into a cool clay pot to be ready to spread on the breakfast bread. Now, it was time to tend to the Tabbouleh. On their way back up to the house, would the family forage for tasty things to toss into it? Wild mushrooms and mint leaves would be a nice surprise.

What an ancient blessing this bulgur parched wheat was, Rhoda realized as she carried a container of soaked and dried grains down from the roof. Then after cracking and packing them, another long term supply of speedy food would be ready, needing only to be quickly softened in water. They had been doubly grateful to have this fast food for travel on their recent flight from Jerusalem, knowing the city was going to be destroyed.

Meanwhile, far away in the celestial galaxies, Jesus, the rejected cosmic King had counted 40 Earth years since returning in His ancient glory to His Father's flaming sapphire throne. Having been given all power and authority in heaven and Earth, and the commission to judge every human soul who ever lived, it was now time to activate the vengeance he had pronounced during His terrestrial visitation. His citizens had said, "We will not have this Man to rule over us!" and He had stated that the King would send his armies and destroy those murderers and burn up their city.[150]

Now it was necessary for Him to fulfill His own predictions and implement all the words He had spoken since it is impossible for God to lie. As Commander of all the armies of the universe, He would requisition Rome this time, just as He had utilized Babylon to destroy the first temple. Clearly, it was written by Daniel the Prophet that He had sent His angel,

Gabriel, to say that Messiah would come and be killed before the second temple would be destroyed. Why else had He wept over the city saying;

> "O Jerusalem, Jerusalem, the one who kills the prophets and stones those who are sent to her! How often I wanted to gather your children together as a hen gathers her chicks under her wings, but you were not willing! See! Your house (temple) is left to you desolate"[151]

Emerging unseen through the cloud cover over Rome, both Peter's angel and Paul's angel had been briefed in heaven for their supreme assignments. Finally, it was time for the two great apostles' last tortures to end in eternal triumph! Soon they would arrive at the heavenly throne, escaping both their own agonies and the horrors ready to happen in the Holy City. All the angels had heard they were about to receive their crowns and rewards, not to mention their mansions. Excitement was building for a vast welcoming party of converts, martyrs and all the true prophets and good kings of Israel, including David himself.

"Isn't there something remotely familiar about this place?" Peter's angel asked Paul's as they both flew down past Capitoline Hill toward the Tullian prison (Mamertine). "Didn't we both see this ghastly dungeon begin as a rocky quarry three thousand years ago?" "Yes, I think you're right," answered

Paul's angel. "But the landscape was littered with them in those days when the Nephilm roamed the Earth, before and after the global flood. Only they had the superhuman strength to build with huge stones, which is why you and I both see their houses, temples and pyramids still standing all over the world, thousands of years after the flood devastated the Earth."

With wings shimmering in the sun, Peter's angel hovered in the huddle a while longer, repeating an ancient complaint, "If only some of the other angels hadn't fallen for Lucifer's revolution! He was always beguiling us with his music and dazzling us with his jeweled splendor. Boasting of his plan for this planet, but being the only extra-terrestrial intelligence from God, we were just supposed to watch over the new Earth race." Paul's angel recoiled as he recalled how Lucifer as Satan used his captive angels to build his kingdom by changing their bodies to have sex with human women, producing new hybrids to corrupt the original creation of the Most High.[152]

"Oh, please don't remind me!" exclaimed Paul's angel, feeling frustration rising. "How I yearn for the time when all the saints are safely home with us and this age-old war with the demons is ended. As the day of the Lord comes, we will defeat these Dragon angels once and for all. Hallelujah!" "True! I too can hardly wait for that day!" agreed Peter's angel. "But for now, I have to strengthen Peter in this prison, so that he may astound his torturers and bring glory to God." Then, parting from that part of the planet, Paul's angel bid farewell and soared up to Spain, where he would connect and protect the great Kingdom Ambassador through the end phase of his homegoing.

Back in Rome, Peter was now being dropped into the deep dungeon of the most monstrous prison ever known. Thousands of years old and never cleaned, it was dark as night, with the smell of hell, its fatal fumes having poisoned untold numbers of prisoners, driving even famous warriors stark, raving mad! So how could Simon Peter, standing chained to a stone post, unable ever to lie down, possibly survive even a week? And how was it that inexplicably he kept on enduring month after impossible month? Everyone knew it had to be only by some supernatural power source (but of course, his angel was invisible to them). So by the time he was still incredibly living after nine whole months, Peter had converted not only his two jailers but also 27 other prisoners to Messiah! Had Peter not written in his letter from Babylon "...do not think it strange concerning the fiery trial which is to try you, but rejoice, that you partake of Christ's sufferings, that when His glory is revealed, you may also be glad with exceeding joy."[153]

After this, Nero had him taken out to the Circus Maximus and crucified upside down, at Peter's own request, feeling unworthy to die as his Lord did. Thereafter it would be known as "Nero's Cross" a symbol which, to him, meant the peace that would come when Christianity and Judaism were destroyed with only Emperor worship and Pantheism remaining. Though he would be forced to commit suicide in 68 A.D., the Roman

Legions later invaded Jerusalem with Nero's "peace sign" ☮ on their banners and standards. It was the symbol of overthrowing Israel's God.

But for Paul, there would be no cross at all, only beheading, which was the special privilege just for those few who had Roman citizenship. Having returned from Spain, he was arrested in Rome and lost all legal appeals because by now, his faith had been declared illegal (Religio Illicito). Fearing for their own lives, all friends deserted him. Only Luke, his constant companion, was faithful to the end. At last, the greatest quest, adventure, and long perilous journey had arrived at its goal. Rabbi Saul's (aka Paul) small, badly scarred body had survived stoning to death, total shipwreck, five times of 39 whip lashings, arena riots, multiple years in prison chains, trials before kings, divine power healings, casting a psychic demon out of a slave girl chaneller, escaping many murder plots, spiritually overpowering sorcerers, and an earthquake jailbreak. which he refused to escape in order to bring salvation to the guard and his family who joined Lydia's group at Philippi.[154]

Paul's final prison had been in the same gruesome place as Peter's. Being led out of the city on the major Ostian Road, he seemed to the crowds who were flowing in and out of town, to be only another criminal being led away as were many others–a usual sight. The executioners leading him stopped. The block was put down and Paul laid his head on it. The sword or axe was raised and the head of the great ambassador for the King of the Universe rolled on the ground! But his crown was waiting in a different dimension along with a new body. Which is why he could say "to die is gain."[155]

By 71 A.D, it seemed like the whole world had radically changed. At the east end of the Mediterranean, still in Caesarea, Cornelius the Centurion, now old and retired, had just made a very big decision. He would move from the sea coast across the river to Pella. Having mourned the executions of Peter, his beloved mentor, and Paul in 67 A.D., he longed to spend his final years in the spiritual comfort of the large community of Yeshua's followers on the other side, the east bank of the Jordan.

In the fall, having gathered all of his family, friends, servants and other converts who wanted to go with him, he sent word to the elders of the local synagogue. Over 40 years earlier, having given his own money to have it built for them, they had even commended him to Jesus! Approaching the assembled elders, all draped in their tallits, Cornelius left the horses, baggage and whole entourage that was waiting outside under trees which were thirsting for the early winter rains. Embracing his frail friends with unstoppable tears, the old soldier and benefactor asked for their blessing. Then he solemnly said, "I have the privilege of a military escort and have been advised on the safest route from Galilee to Decapolis. I have had access to full reports of these years of siege and atrocities in Jerusalem. I want to give the complete story to the believers in Pella, so that we might mourn and pray together. I'm sure you understand, and I will never forget your kindness to me."[156]

Meanwhile in Pella, Rhoda had received word that the large company with Cornelius wanted to share the High Holy Days there, saying that his servants would help with the reaping of fields and orchards for the great harvest festival. "Tabernacles" was the most joyful of all the Lord's appointed feasts. Its preparation required the happy participation of all generations. Gathering of all the final yearly fruits, nuts, and grains was underway but that wasn't the most fun part for the children. Young of all ages were asking the elders, "Please, can we go cut the palm branches and willows by the brooks and help build our family sukkah?" What they loved was eating and sleeping outdoors under the stars and full moon for a week in a sort of tree house on the ground.[157]

Little girls were pleading with their mothers and big sisters, "Ima, can we please borrow some really big baskets? This year, we want to collect the flowers and dried fruits to hang on strings and decorate inside our sukkah." Echoing the laughter of the little ones, autumn breezes were blowing through the hills and valleys of Pella. The cooler air was reminding everyone that the time of the winter storage season was coming. But now, suddenly spotting Cornelius' long moving caravan winding up slowly in the distance, all the families started running downhill to help with the hospitality of his welcome.

After unloading and settling in, Cornelius and his company remembered to thank Rhoda for finding them an ideal house, even with a valley view of vineyards. Also outside and on the roof, the young men had built a large sukkah for him, hoping to visit and hear Roman war stories and adventures from the early days of the old Centurion's military service. So for seven days they all rejoiced together in the festival…singing, dancing, eating, drinking, worshipping, praying and reading the Word of God.

Children loved to wave palm branches by day and look up through them at night to see the stars above their leafy roof. Then they curled up in warm, wooly soft sheepskins to sleep in the chilly night air on the ground inside their flimsy family shelters. After the coals of the cooking fires had died down and the clay ovens for bread had cooled off, they were still snug and cozy until the cocks crowed at dawn.

On the last day, when the whole congregation was studying the Holy Scriptures together, one of the young men asked about a prophecy of the future kingdom. "Wasn't Tabernacles just a commemoration of the Israelites camping out in the desert 40 years after their exodus from Egyptian slavery? Then how odd that God told Zechariah, the prophet that when Messiah returns as King over all the Earth, He will command rulers of ALL nations to come to Jerusalem every year to keep the Feast of Tabernacles and threatens them with drought if they don't!" For an answer, one of the elders, feeling a little quizzical himself, guessed that it would be because God Himself was "tabernacling" with us, since Jesus' title of Immanuel means "God with us."[158]

Now Sukkot was over. All the outdoor shelters had been taken apart, provisions for winter had been stored and everybody waited for the early rains to arrive. Having called together all the assembly of Pella, Cornelius had waited until this quiet time to retell the recent horror story of Jerusalem. Trying to keep his composure, he simply began to recite the facts in a controlled voice. "As you recall, many of those who started the revolt were unemployed. After 43 years of building King Herod's vast enlargement of the Temple, suddenly in 64 A.D. it was finished and thousands of people were thrown out of work. Ruthless resentment began spreading and the revolutionary Zealots used it to stir up a great armed insurrection against the government.

"Amazingly," he continued to explain, "the rebels repelled the Romans and succeeded in occupying Jerusalem in 66, but then fought among themselves since they lacked leadership, discipline, training and preparation. So, in 67, Vespasian, with the 10th Legion from Syria, invaded Galilee and going south to Jerusalem, destroyed rebel forces on the way. Afterward, Titus surrounded the city with four legions, allowing the religious pilgrims to enter it for Passover at the Temple. But he refused to let them back out. Soon food and water ran out. Trapped inside the walls like caged animals, there was horrendous starvation, sickness, death and even cannibalism. When some escaped through the secret underground tunnels, the Romans caught them coming out."

By this point, Cornelius heard soft sobbing punctuated with loud wails coming from the assembled listeners, but in a voice often choked with sorrow, he was still able to continue. "Inside the sealed off walls of Jerusalem, the great massacre created a mass grave. The Roman legions had to climb over heaps of dead bodies to keep on killing men, women, children and priests in a random frenzy of extermination. Some Jews committed suicide and some were hung on the walls, but the hills surrounding the city became forests of crosses. With 500 people a day being crucified, the five month siege resulted in over one million Jews killed and 97,000 sold as slaves, exiled from their homeland to the foreign nations of the world."

Now a look of exasperation crossed Cornelius' face as he was finishing his report. "Worst of all, the Romans were led in this war by a commander from Egypt who was himself a Jew! Some said that Titus wanted to save the Temple to make it into a pagan Roman pantheon with emperor worship. But at one point, a soldier threw a burning stick into its wall and the gold began to melt. Because King Herod had beautified the Temple with so much gold, the soldiers threw down all the huge stones to get it, making Jesus' prediction come true that not one stone would be left on another." With a great sigh, Cornelius continued to the end. "It is desolate, all of the trees cut down. Now it's a desert with all signs of beauty laid waste. It was leveled to the ground to make people think it had never been inhabited as a city."[159]

After hearing it all, the whole congregation of Pella mourned together, especially over family and friends who had died by refusing to escape because of disbelief in Yeshua's prophecy of destruction, or because they were priests devoted to the temple. They remembered Daniel the prophet had written a message hundreds of years before, given by the angel Gabriel, that the second temple would be destroyed after Messiah came and was killed, "but not for Himself." Then they all agreed that it would appear to the world as if the Kingdom of God would never come now and that Israel would have no future. But their tears turned to hope when Cornelius announced, "Yet we know the Word of God says Messiah must sit on a throne in Jerusalem and rule over all the Earth only from that city!" "Yes, Halleluyah!" agreed Rhoda. "So all the seemingly impossible promises of restoration have to happen. But O Lord, how long will it take?"[160]

WHITE HORSE FORCE:
BOOK ONE

WHO CAN MAKE ME A *SUPER-IMMORTAL?*

PART SIX

PREPARE FOR APOCALYPSE:
THE STORY OF YOUR BLESSING

26
INVASION OF THE BODY SNATCHER

⁓෧෧⁓

"HA HA HA HARPAZO! HA HA HA HARPAZO! HA HA HA HARPAZO!" The ridge above the river was resounding with shouts. Arms and faces toward the sky, the two brothers were jumping high then rolling on the ground, laughing. Taking turns trying to top each other, they were creating a game of imagining the fantastic event of the future, namely, "What could it be like when Messiah invades the atmosphere to snatch our bodies off the Earth?"

"Suppose I'm in prison for refusing to say 'Caesar is Lord,'" said one brother, "and just as they chain me in the dungeon, I fly up through the roof, glowing and disappear!" After a good laugh and a few more leaps, the youngest brother described his scene. "I am about to be burned at the stake for not denying Jesus. They've tied me with ropes to a post and they're piling up wood around my feet and legs while spitting insults and profanity against the Name of their Creator. But, instantly, their heads are spinning as they watch a magnetic force pull me up in the clouds to meet the Lord in the air!"

"That's good," interrupted the other brother, "But what about this ending instead to make our enemies even more dumbfounded: They go ahead and light the fire and watch you burn to a pile of ashes on the ground. Then all of a sudden the ashes start forming into a super-immortal body which flies up in the sky before their very eyes!" Hilarious rejoicing by both of them followed!

Often, they would hear people ridicule the resurrection and the crazy, preposterous idea of a sky invader snatching up bodies, dead or alive and changing them into a race of new immortals. But hadn't Apostle Paul (Rabbi Saul), used their own Greek word HARPAZO (snatch forcefully), when he described this amazing event which the Lord had specifically revealed to him?[161] This was the great, unique hope that strengthened them to endure all the persecutions of the empire.

But now, their joy was to be cut short. Their older brother had just arrived and started mocking and imitating them with a disgusted look on his face. "Don't you two even know that no Harpazo can happen anytime soon because Jerusalem and the temple are destroyed?" "So what?" the younger two declared, "Yeshua said to watch because He was coming at a time we don't think He will, and that only a wicked servant would say 'my Lord delays His coming.'"[162]

The middle brother, at 14, was big for his age and despite a limp from a childhood accident, he felt that his red hair and size made up for it. Grabbing this bully down in a wrestling hold, he sarcastically shouted, "All right, big brother. Since you know so much because you're 19 going on 30 then answer this question! Apostle Paul wrote that we followers of Jesus will rule the world, right?"[163] "Right," agreed the eldest, loosing the hold and catching his breath. "So, after He invades Earth's space to snatch our bodies up to the dwellings in heaven, how will we get back down here to rule?"

Bowing down in jest, big brother conceded, "Well, I guess I'll have to let you win this time, because right now, nobody can answer that question." Then the youngest, a nine year old, after pointing out the grass stains on the two wrestlers' clothing, looked up at them with that little kid big smile saying, "I can't imagine the answer either, but when we find out, I'll bet it'll be really astounding!"

While enjoying the landscape of Laodicea, a very wealthy city in the Roman province of Asia Minor (Turkey), the brothers ran through a lush green valley on their way home. In the distance, they saw the two converging rivers that controlled trade flowing toward the seacoast. The ships, as well as three great roads nearby, carried exclusive goods produced only in this area. In particular, were the prized tunics made from super soft raven black wool from their distinctive local sheep, not to mention some unique medicinal items as well.

Growing up in one of the richest centers of the ancient world, the boys didn't have much to compare it with and yearned to someday go on a quest to the far-flung corners of the empire. Little did they know, it might begin to happen sooner than they ever dreamed! Meanwhile, some sort of mysterious intrigue had been going on at their house. An unknown visitor, a courier, had arrived along with the pastor of their congregation to announce an alarming summons being sent to seven cities. Some unique new supernatural book had been brought to Ephesus and the leaders of all seven congregations were being commanded to go there and hear it.

But the three sons had slipped up the outdoor stairway unawares, and lying on the floor of the balcony, they had overheard everything said below in the courtyard. Quietly they crawled into an upstairs bedroom and closed the door. Huddling together like conspirators, the eldest began in a loud whisper; "Listen to this! I've thought of a great plan! We can go to Ephesus with the pastor instead of our parents, because they're always too busy with business anyway. All we need to do is offer to be his servants and help with everything on the way!"

Grabbing some wine-dipped bread for breakfast the next morning, the brothers hurried to load the pastor's baggage.

Just as they had hoped, it was easy to persuade their parents to let them take the trip as an educational experience. Being a rich merchant, their father was able to provide not only a carriage and horses for the 100 mile trip, but also insisted on sending along gifts of the famous glossy black wool tunics. So the three boys were off on their great adventure, having no idea how greatly shocking it would turn out to be!

27
DOOM OF THE GLOBAL GODDESS

_ᘐᘑ_

O ff on their adventure, the boys were on a quest, for what, they knew not. But just being out, moving fast on one of those great Roman roads, surrounded by all types of people, animals and soldiers, felt suspenseful and unpredictable. Heading west to one of the greatest seaports, they realized this road connected all the way back east to the Euphrates, Babylon and the Silk Road to China. For much of the way, the brothers wanted to walk on ahead, leading the horses, so as to talk freely, away from the pastor back in the carriage.

"Don't you think we can persuade him to let us see what Ephesus is most famous for, the great temple of Artemis (Diana)?" asked the redheaded middle brother. "How can he refuse?" replied the eldest, "since it is one of the Seven

Wonders of The World and we can say it will be an educational experience without defiling ourselves by going inside it." But even as he said this, there were other attractions he had been secretly pondering in his mind. . . without even trying to resist.

Finally, after traveling for over a week, they saw the road was becoming more and more congested as they got closer to the city. Not only because of the Pan-Ionian Games (rival of the Olympics) but people of all ages, classes and cultures were drawn like a magnet to the splendor of that huge temple of the world renowned great goddess. For most of them, it would be a once-in-a-lifetime thrill.

As the pastor was waiting in the carriage and the boys approached the temple grounds, suddenly screams erupted behind them. Like a swimmer plunging through waves in a storm, a desperate man was pushing his way past swarms of strangers. Like many others, the brothers barely missed being knocked down by the jabbing blows of his elbows!

"I'm going to brace myself on the base of this statue" said the oldest brother, "and you two climb up on my shoulders and hold onto it to see what happened." Getting up to the highest vantage point, the smallest brother yelled down "It's murder! Bloody murder! I see a man on the ground with stab wounds all over, lying in a pool of blood surrounded by people staring."

But just then, in the other direction, the running, sweating knife-wielder had reached his goal. Safe at last! He had

entered the precnct of the protected circle of criminals surrounding Artemis' temple to whom the goddess was sworn
to offer asylum. Needless to say, a large collection of killers,
robbers and rapists had found refuge in the shadows of her
sanctuary for untold ages.

There it was: The enormous, white marble building
looming outside the city in all of its gleaming glory. One
hundred majestic columns rose up over 55 feet high to support a roof 340 feet long. Gold leaf, bright paint and beautiful sculpture adorned the temple of this famous fertility
sex-goddess, which was four times larger than the Parthenon
in Athens. The cult of Artemis brought many thousands
here yearly to perform her sacred rites with a large staff
of eunuchs, priests and virgins. Also, like most temples, it
functioned as an international bank and magical arts flourished everywhere in the vicinity as well. But the reality of
the magnificence of this structure was only exceeded by the
vile depravity of the worship within.

Running back as fast as possible to the carriage, the boys
breathlessly told the pastor about the horror they had just
witnessed. Calming them down with a jug of cool water, the
pastor began to unwrap a special treat he had been saving.
"Oh look!" they exclaimed, wide eyed "it's that wonderful
gingerbread from Isle of Rhodes that everyone in the empire
craves!"

"Yes, indeed," added the voice of an approaching
stranger, as he came closer to that alluring aroma of spices

and honey, "and they all send ships there just to load up on this prized possession!" As he gladly accepted the delicious bread slice now being offered to him, the distinguished visitor introduced himself. "If you are by any chance the pastor of the Laodicea congregation, then I'm here to escort you to the villa of Aquila and Priscilla, where the leaders from the other six cities have already gathered. Since the courier had told us you'd have three boys with you, I guessed you might be sightseeing in this area. Having seen one of the more unsavory surprises of this supreme metropolis, you'll probably be glad to get away from your ordeal at this world wonder. Just follow me. I'll ride on my horse ahead of yours and lead you to the awaiting assembly."

As it turned out, their new escort was a former philosophy teacher from Athens. Many years before, feeling challenged by Paul's speech there at the Aeropagus (Mars Hill),[164] he later followed Paul to the congregation in Ephesus. Now, a large Mediterranean villa was beginning to come into view. Its white walls and roof of cascading terra cotta tiles were perfectly offset by the bluest shimmering sky. Tall cypress tree sentinels surrounded the house, pointing heavenward.

As soon as the crunch of the carriage wheels was heard on the crushed shell entrance way, all three brothers bounded out to survey the scene. Since Aquila was away at the marketplace buying more provisions, their gracious hostess, Priscilla opened the door. With a warm welcoming smile on her face, she gave them the traditional greeting of a hug and holy kiss in the name of Jesus the Messiah. Wearing a colorful, long-draped Greek gown, her simply braided hair was neatly pinned back. With minimal jewelry, she still looked lovely, even at age 75! Her voice was as soothing as ever.

Turning to leave, Priscilla said, "I hear you've just seen the great goddess temple! After you've settled in your rooms, please come down and join us for dinner under the pergola. Afterward, I'll tell you what's going to happen to her in the end time, which I just heard in last night's apocalypse reading. But now I need to help in the kitchen with seasoning the stuffing for the fresh eggplants Aquila is bringing from the market. So just rest on the balcony and I'll send up some glasses of cold water with spoons of our apricot jam."

The year was 95 A.D., and 60 years after returning to space from Earth, Jesus had just taken one of His founding ambassadors on a time travel vision. Being told to write down this detailed picture of the future end time events, he was afterward released from the Roman prison island of Patmos. Now well over the age of 90, Yohanan (John) was the last of the twelve apostles still alive on Earth. Having long been the elder pastor of the congregation at Ephesus, he made his way back with the precious manuscript to the familiar meeting place, the favored villa of Aquila and Priscilla. Each night, he and others had been reading aloud from the new book of Revelation, but this night he excused himself after dinner to rest and allow for discussion among the listeners.

Caressed by a soft Mediterranean breeze and filled with delicious food, all the guests leaned on their cushions, reaching up to pick grapes from the pergola, anxious to listen to Priscilla's promised teaching. "Throughout history," she began "every culture has had its own goddess, sometimes more than one. As you know, Ephesus has Artemis, Athens has Athena, Rome has Venus, Egypt has Isis, Babylon has Ishtar, Crete has Gaia, and Israel used to have Ashtoreth (Astarte). These goddesses all claim to be the powers behind love, sex, fertility, wisdom, war and even mother Earth. Often their temples and shrines are the most opulent.

"But when God's people insisted on worshipping the 'Queen of Heaven'[165] it brought about the downfall and exile of Israel with the destruction of the first temple (Solomon's). But now, Yeshua the Messiah has revealed to us what will happen to this global goddess in the end of the age just before His return. She will be linked to both Rome and Babylon and be involved with governments and world trade. Pictured as the mother of prostitutes and abominations of the Earth, she is lavishly clothed in royal garments with jewels and pearls, holding a gold goblet. She is said to be drunk with the blood of the saints and martyrs of Jesus, which we all know about continuing from the time of Nero and other Caesars."[166]

However, Jesus said, "The Holy Spirit would come to glorify Him[167] but these goddesses always demand sanctuaries and shrines built in their names to glorify themselves. Then, as fallen angels, they do magic miracles to lure people into worshipping them. That's why we know that if Jesus' mother Mary, or Mary Magdalene, or Martha and Mary of Bethany ever appeared to any of us, they would never ask for any shrine to be built in their names; nor accept worship of themselves or any praise for healings or miracles in their own names, nor would any of the other saints. That's how we can discern spiritual imposters from the beautiful side of evil. All glory goes only to God the Father and His Son, Yeshua, the Messiah. That's why it is written that Jesus is the only mediator between God and humanity and there is no other name by which we must be saved![168]

"But in our new Revelation book of the end times, this goddess is seen sitting on a seven-headed leopard with ten horns. This represents the final world empire of Satan's anointed king, who is like a reincarnated Nimrod coming back up out of the abyss from ancient times. The question is, why do the ten powers of this dragon kingdom hate the city of Rome and burn it up in the end?[169] And since this final false messiah will be a superhuman superman, energized by Satan, no mortal man can kill him. Not until the real Son of God returns will he be destroyed.[170] Now, I'll just let you all discuss and decide how the rest of the details fit together with the future prophecies in the Hebrew Bible."

No sooner had Priscilla stopped speaking and sat down, than the whole table erupted in lively debate; being Jews and Greeks, what else would they do? But at the far end of the pergola, in the shadows past the few flickering oil lamps, the oldest brother saw his chance to slip away unnoticed, even by his younger brothers. Once outside the villa, he paced restlessly in the moonlight. His heart was churning and yearning, visualizing the thrills he could have not far away at the great Pan-Ionian Games. But how would he be able to get away? A careful plan and good excuse needed to be thought out as quickly as possible!

28
RETURN OF THE LIVING DEAD

———⁀ᖾ᎐ᕝ⁀———

Long before dawn, being certain that everyone was still asleep, the oldest brother tucked a note under the arm of the youngest and quietly easing out of the room, pushed another one under the pastor's door. Both of them said the same thing, "Please forgive me, but I need to go up to Smyrna to visit a cousin there. I'll be back in a week to explain and hear the reading of the new book."

For many centuries, the Pan-Ionian League of twelve cities had sponsored a festival of games, sacrifices and sacred rites devoted to Poseidon, so this was to be a forbidden adventure. "You only live once," he thought to himself. It was a beautiful day as he approached the spectacular scene, mingling in the crowds and even sampling some of the sacrifices. He had always been more attracted to men than women but in Greece, that wasn't unusual. The boys and young men were always going around naked in their gymnasiums and athletic events like the Olympics and other games which were religious traditions dedicated to gods and goddesses.

But he had never yet yielded to this desire, knowing what God had said about it.[171] Just then, at a distance, he noticed one of the athletes staring at him, whose eyes were actually glittering and hypnotic. Riveted and unable to move, he just stood there in a clump of pine trees until the man ran up swiftly and pressed his muscled, bare body tightly against him, leering like a satyr.

Gripped with a fear of rising lust, the elder brother forcibly twisted his head down to look at the ground, away from those eyes! Then with every ounce of resistance he had, he slid down the tree trunk to escape and took off running toward the road to Smyrna. Still sweating in a panic of his own passion, he could hear the loud laughing, mocking and obscene voice of the athlete trailing off in the distance. As he finally reached the road to finish the rest of the 35 miles, he wondered if this escapade was going to haunt him forever. What had started as an exhilarating day had ended in an encounter he would never be able to forget, hoping it was not going to torment him with erotic fantasies.

Smyrna was located on a deep gulf of the Mediterranean Sea with a magnificent harbor. It was a great trade city, rich in wine, a model of beautiful planning since about 400 B.C.

Straight, wide streets stretched from the sea to the foot-
hills, with splendid and stupendous temples for all the top
gods and goddesses of the empire. Known as the birthplace
of Homer, it was the glory of Asia with a famous stadium,
library and theater. By claiming to be not only first in beauty,
but also in Caesar worship, it was a perilous place for the
assembly of the Lord Jesus.

It had taken some searching to find his cousin's house,
since he hadn't been there in years, but after hugs and greetings of "Maranatha!" he was welcomed inside. Looking
around, he was shocked at the change and condition of their
family dwelling. They were more than poor, now they were
destitute. After his wife served them all a tasty but meager
meal, the two daughters, ages seven and eleven, were looking
up admiringly at this newly arrived nineteen year old. "We
don't go up to heaven and that's the end of us," exclaimed
the older girl, twirling a lock of her long brown hair. "We're
all coming back with the Kingdom to rule the Earth for
Jesus!"[172] "Yes," agreed her little sister, "so we don't mind
losing everything and being poor now, because we'll own
the whole world!"[173]

Then sitting their visitor down on a well-worn cushion,
they both came close to his ear saying, "You know what?
We've cast demons out of some of the pagan children and
prayed for sick people like Jesus said to do using His Name[174]
and they began coming to our congregation!" But both girls
confessed, "Sometimes we cry about having our furniture

and toys taken away, but we'll think up new ones to make ourselves, either here or in heaven."[175]

With a mixture of resolve, sadness and joy on his face, the cousin explained, "Now that the empire has made us illegal, we're civil outcasts with no rights. The official privileges granted to Jews were taken away when they decided Christians were a different group, even though we had to go to the synagogues to learn about God and hear His written messages." While washing and drying their few remaining dishes, his wife added, "So now we have no exemption from Caesar worship. We never know when we might be betrayed, even by friends or family, Jews or Gentiles, and the authorities demand we burn some incense and say 'Caesar is Lord' to receive an official certificate allowing us to go on living. Otherwise, we might be burned at the stake and that's why they looted our wealth and confiscated our belongings–as a warning."[176]

Drawing his family together in his arms, the cousin concluded, "We're not reminiscing about what we had, but concentrating on the challenge Jesus gave us in His new book, which our pastor heard in Ephesus. Yeshua said to us here in Smyrna that He knew of our poverty but that we are rich. Although Satan may put us in prison a short time, if we are faithful to death we will be given a crown of life.[177] If Messiah does not return in our lifetime, then when He does, we will return as the living from the dead. The power of Christ's resurrection is everything! Without it, we have no future. He didn't return from the grave as a re-animated corpse and therefore, neither will we!"

"Speaking of the return of the living dead," replied the oldest brother. "Priscilla was telling us that this new book depicts Nimrod coming back up out of the abyss." "True," answered the cousin, "it could be him, because in the books of the ancient prophets, God calls this ultimate wicked one the Assyrian from the land of Nimrod[178] and the king of Babylon and also a prince from somewhere in the Roman empire."[179] "Well," agreed the visitor, "we've got plenty of Assyrians here in the empire now. Everyone knows it was the 10th Roman Legion in Syria mostly that destroyed Jerusalem."

For some reason, although it was getting late and they were both yawning, his cousin didn't want to stop talking and launched into a bedtime horror story. Not wanting to waken his wife and daughters, he scooted his cushion closer, and speaking in a soft whisper asked; Want to hear some more details of the new Apocalypse?" The house guest nodded, putting his hand behind his ear to catch every word. "Have you ever heard people ask 'if there's a good God, why doesn't He stop the evil?'" began the cousin. "Well, this is the book that answers that question.

"God's problem is that the evil is done by people whom He created with a free will and He's hoping they will change their minds and stop doing it. But there is a limit and He does have a deadline. It's called 'The Day Of The Lord,' spoken of many times in future prophecy scriptures. Instead of the waters of a flood like Noah's which was painless, the next time will be fire! For instance, this revelation shows that people will still curse God and refuse to stop doing evil, even after one third of the world has been killed by a 200 million demonic army from the underworld! It depicts them as a hybrid cavalry of creatures with supernatural powers for massive death. They ride up out of the abyss by orders of four ancient archon angels who have been bound (like the Titans) for eons at the Euphrates river.[180]

"But wait till you hear this," the cousin continued, "Before these 200 million monstrosities attack, Jesus gives His destroyer angel, Abaddon, the key to the abyss and sends him down to open it. An immense cloud of black smoke comes up full of weird, mutant scorpions which bite and sting all the God-haters for five months of total torture, but they're not allowed to die."[181] "I can guess why," interrupted the visitor, "because God knows how infinitely worse the eternal lake of fire is!"

"Correct," agreed his host. "And that's only during the fifth and sixth angel trumpets, which is way before the seven finals bowls of wrath!" "WHOA! I'm getting dumbfounded with disbelief by all this!" protested the other cousin. "Not until I get back to the villa and hear John read what he saw himself, can I accept that this will all be real, but thanks for the awesome preview. Goodnight!"

As his skin scraped on the roughly woven floor sleeping mat and pulling his outer garment up over his head, the oldest brother rolled over toward the wall. Not wanting yet to think about anything he'd just heard or anything else that had happened earlier in the day, he was hoping a nightmare wouldn't strike. But it was of no avail, as his mind and emotions were reeling with re-enactments of what he nearly did at the Pan-Ionian games. Guilt and remorse mingled with lingering lust to climax the craving. Had he somehow opened a portal in the spirit realm just by looking and being touched?

Suddenly, an unseen hostile presence wanted to enter his body. It pushed him over onto his back, and began pressing its heavy, invisible weight down on top of him, trying to force its way into his body, while at the same time attempting to strangle and suffocate the life out of him! Unable to breathe, this malevolent demon was making it impossible for him to cry out. He was resisting it with all the strength of his soul when finally, by the grace of God, it just stopped. Lying there limp and grateful, something was telling him this spirit might be more dangerous and vicious than if he had been with a woman instead.[182]

Early the next morning, after a little erratic sleep, he told his cousin, "I've got to talk to you privately! Can you walk with me down to the beach and I'll buy you some breakfast of those little circular sesame seed breads the harbor vendors always sell. Then I'll give you a lot more, along with some cheeses and fruit to take back to your family for lunch." Not long after they

had set off on their walk, the younger cousin desperately confessed everything he had done the day before. Putting a com-
passionate arm on his shoulder, the older man promised to pray
for him. As the prayer of deliverance and comfort along with
scriptures of forgiveness, the heavenly Spirit language flowed
from his lips as the younger cousin felt a great soul cleansing
taking place. Afterwards, he thanked him sincerely.[183]

Continuing on their walk, the older asked, "Would you
like to know the origin of your impulse? Where the idea came
from?" Feeling ambivalent but curious, the elder brother
nodded yes anyway. "Satan hates babies!" proclaimed the
cousin with disgust. "In the beginning, God had told His
people to multiply and fill the Earth and have dominion.
That's why it is said 'the hand that rocks the cradle rules
the world.' However, the devil devised a plan to give himself and his fallen angels dominion instead. They would
capture Earth women to create a race of giant demigods,[184]
and then teach sex with the same gender and animals to prevent offspring." Also, they promoted sex abuse of children
to ruin them for normal marriage and to perpetuate genera-
tional curses, not to mention luring them into witchcraft at
an early age."

"Now I'm beginning to understand," replied the other
cousin with amazement. "The ultimate goal is to corrupt,
control and destroy the human population of planet Earth,
because they were created in God's image.[185] Instead Satan
wanted to produce creatures in his image which would be the

261

seed of the serpent or children of the wicked one, as Jesus called them." "That's exactly right," agreed the older cousin. "Now you know why the gods and goddesses always wanted baby sacrifices as well as human blood sacrifices."[186]

Surrounded by the busy sights and sounds of the harbor, they chose their food from the street vendors and quickly walked away to climb a grassy hill in the distance. Plucking some tree leaves for plates, they spread out their breakfast on a large rock while scanning the lovely panorama. Hungrily chewing his sesame roll, along with some cheese and olives, the older cousin asked the younger; "Do you remember when Jesus said the time of His return would be like the days of Noah and the days of Lot?[187] I'm told this new revelation book says at that time Jerusalem will be spiritually like Sodom and Egypt, meaning homosexuality and idols will be everywhere![188]

"So it turns out," he continued, "that the Sodomites weren't the worst people after all. Jerusalem will be.[189] "Hundreds of years ago, God told Ezekiel the prophet the whole history of Jerusalem and said that it will be worse than Sodom, and that He is going to restore Sodom when He restores Jerusalem and Samaria." As his breakfast companion gasped at this shocking news, the rest of the story would be even more astounding! "But then before the Lord Yeshua Messiah comes back, all three cities will be invaded, with captives taken into exile. Now here's the amazing ending. He brings all three back together. Jerusalem's captives along with the captives of Sodom and Samaria, saying Jerusalem should be ashamed and never open her mouth again!"[190]

Hearing all that, the younger man nearly choked on his bread! "Who has ever heard about this?" he asked, "since Sodom is always used as an example of total destruction. On the other hand, I recall that Jesus said even they would have repented and remained if He had gone there to do His miracles." "Yes," added the cousin, "and he cursed the Galilee town of Capernaum because they didn't and said that at the Judgment the men of Sodom would rise up and condemn them.[191] I guess all this is going to happen to keep Jerusalem humble when the Kingdom is established there because, after all, Sodom had no written scriptures, no oracles of God."

"The odd thing is that this particular sin of same sex unions seems to be cause for celebration in the end time," remarked the family man. "God described it long ago to Isaiah and Jeremiah the prophets, saying, 'They parade their sin like Sodom, they do not hide it, nor can they blush.'"[192] "Astonishing!" answered the 19 year old, "imagine a parade of adulterers or thieves or drunkards!"

As he packed up the leftovers, putting them in a basket with the rest of the gift food in his shoulder bag, the older man concluded; "But you're missing the point. God loves restoration and this rebuilding of Sodom sounds the most improbable of all.[193] When His Kingdom comes to Earth, His powers of transformation will be displayed in Jerusalem, Samaria and even Sodom, like a trophy of grace!" While thanking his cousin for sharing the fascinating prophecies and saying farewell, the eldest brother said, "Do you mind if I just stay down here for the rest of the day and take a walk on the beach?" "Not at all, but of course we'll expect you back for dinner. And don't forget to forgive that young athlete and pray for him."

Now that he was left alone, the young man stretched out on the grass above the bay, feeling infused with peace. Staring up at the majestic procession of sculpted clouds, his spirit erupted in praise to the Lord for calming the turmoil of his soul. He was ready for unconditional surrender to the One Who would never leave him or forsake him and could be trusted to direct his life.[194] Then, in a moment of spiritual hunger for more, he asked Jesus to baptize him with the Holy Spirit, knowing he was going to need the power, discernment and self-control.[195]

Expecting a new, mysterious language to begin flowing out of his mouth, he yielded to the thrilling sensation of lightning and warm honey being poured all over, inside and out! But others had told him of different experiences, so this one was wonderfully surprising and sealed the love and commitment in his heart.[196] As he began climbing down the hill to the shore, he really felt for the first time he was truly born again.[197] Reaching the beach, he just walked slowly and humbly, contemplating everything. Then unexpectedly, he found himself saying "Holy Spirit, it would really be a blessing if you gave me some special token to remember this day." Not knowing what to expect, he continued walking with his head down, looking at the sand. Then it happened, suddenly his eye was drawn to a certain half buried seashell. Quickly bending over, pulling it out and brushing it off, he could hardly believe what he was seeing. There in his hand lay the image of the crucified foot of the Lord Jesus, complete with a large hole near the ankle!

Gasping with gratitude while securing it safely in his belt, he ran and leaped for joy all the way back to the marketplace to buy it a gold chain. Elated with this miracle treasure, he lovingly looped the gold chain through the memorable hole of the shell-foot and attached it around his neck, vowing to use it to tell the good news and declaring out loud, "Now I have an amulet like no other! Halleluyah! Forever it will hang over my heart!"

Still dazed at such a unique answer to prayer, he knew it called for a celebration, so he searched for some of the best things in the market to share a lavish, last feast with his cousin's family. Collecting a donkey, for a fee, he loaded it with fresh, charcoal-grilled fish, several kinds of breads, olives, lemons, and herbs. Choice olive oil, honey, spices, wine, vegetables, rice and fruits were added. To finish off his shopping spree, dates, sweets, cakes, nuts and funny toys and candies for the little girls. Needless to say, by the time he arrived back at the house, leading the donkey, they all were ecstatic and couldn't stop laughing. As they prepared, served and ate the sumptuous, surprise dinner, he anointed the foot-shell with oil and showed it personally to each one. After they all admired it with delight, he told the whole beach story just before bed and ended it with a holy kiss goodnight.

Waking before dawn with an urgency to get back to Ephesus to hear the whole apocalypse, the eldest brother took out one of the wrapped gifts of wool tunics from Laodicea. He tucked in a bag of gold coins and softly slipped out the door after leaving it on a cushion with a goodbye/thank you note. Then dropping the donkey off at the marketplace, he bought provisions for his journey and set off on the excellent Roman road to the south, singing in the Spirit!

29
EXTRA-TERRESTRIAL JERUSALEM

S everal days later, arriving back in Ephesus at the marketplace around noon, the older brother over-heard a group of eight Ethiopians talking to a vendor just shuttering his shop for the midday rest. Surprised that they were actually asking directions to the villa of Aquila and Priscilla, he introduced himself saying, "I just happen to be staying there myself and I'll be happy to personally escort you, just as soon as I buy a few gifts for them and my two younger brothers." Excitedly agreeing, the Ethiopians laughed, adding that since they had come from the climate of Egypt, they wouldn't need to rest from the afternoon heat.

Being told they had left the kingdom of Axum to study at the great Library of Alexandria, he decided to take them on a partial walking tour of Ephesus on the way. Then seeing its famous library, he couldn't help joking about the prestigious scholars who had a secret tunnel underneath which ended at the brothel. After the cynical hilarity subsided, they told him about meeting a Roman Christian traveling merchant who had heard about Apostle John's release from the prison island with a new vision from Jesus. They went on his boat, stopping at Tyre on the way and he promised to pick them up on his way back, when he would stop to hear the new book himself.

What was that loud commotion as they neared the edge of the estate? "HELP! Teacher HELLLLP! He won't stop!" One of the Ethiopians ran like the wind, grabbing the horse and commanding it to stop in the Name of Jesus! Then he stroked its mane, whispering some unknown language in its ear. Sliding off the horse as he thanked the stranger, the panicked rider, who turned out to be the nine year old youngest brother, walked over saying sarcastically, "Oh, so you finally got back! What took you so long?"

Grabbing him in a welcoming bear hug, his eldest brother said, "Why do you want to risk your neck trying to ride some runaway horse, since you haven't learned yet?" "You'll find out at the reading. I'm keeping it secret. Anyway, guess what! Yeshua rode into Jerusalem on a lowly donkey the first time, but He's coming back on a white horse, because that's what conquerors ride!"

Just then, the philosophy teacher come running up to the group, apologizing for letting the boy borrow his horse, not knowing he was inexperienced. Introducing his entire group, including two scribes, the leading pastor of the Ethiopians asked, "Why don't you all come and sit with us in the shade and share the sweets we brought along?" How could they resist that invitation? Joined by some of the other students, they all settled in a circle to get acquainted. A large basket was opened and there were amazing dates stuffed with ground almonds, sesame tahini, honey, coconut and cinnamon! What a heavenly scent and savor!

Looking up at the sun glinting through the crisscross lattice of the palm tree branches, created a lovely spiritual setting for their conversation; so much so that the Ethiopians erupted in spontaneous worship songs in their own language. Where they were sitting on the edge of the villa estate, there was a very deep water well to which the boys were running back and forth with cups of cold water for each guest. Some of the philosophy students had not had a chance to see many black people and they were intrigued by the exotic clothing and graceful posture of these new visitors.

Turning to the teacher, who was dipping his sticky date fingers in water and wiping them on the grass, one of the scribes asked mysteriously, "Do you know the secret code of the Socrates and Plato plan for the so-called 'ideal state'? We discovered it while studying in the great library of Alexandria, because Solon, the sage/poet, from whom they got the story of Atlantis, was an Egyptian.

"Atlantis, which sunk under the ocean named for it, was a very large island/continent, whose control extended into the Mediterranean as far as Italy and Egypt. It was considered a great and wonderful empire, producing a powerful dynasty of kings directly from the god Poseidon. The story goes that their divine, heroic lineage became diluted by mixing with mortals! They attacked all of Europe and Asia, but were swallowed up by the sea and vanished."

"Well, yes" declared the teacher somewhat impatiently, "I'm familiar with most of this, having taught in the park called Academia, after the mythical hero Academus, who had a cult following there and Plato's house and garden were nearby. But, other than the fact that Jesus linked his return to conditions similar to before the flood of Noah, how does Atlantis connect to the future?"

Emphatically answering, the other scribe began to reveal the reason, "It's because they wanted ALL to be ONE, just like Nimrod would try to do after the flood. A small group of elite overlords, which Plato called 'Philosopher Kings' as in the fallen angels and Nephilim that ruled Atlantis, would operate a collective society by mind control. In this ideal state, there would be no love, marriage or family ties. All wives and children would be in common and no one would ever know his own child, but was to imagine they were ALL ONE family. Obviously, there would be no private property and the elite would operate the breeding system to pair together those having offspring worth educating, while the rest would be slaves.

"The ruler," he continued, "was to use constant supervision and manipulation so that nobody could even consider acting as an individual or know how to do so. It would be impossible for anyone to ever think for themselves!"[198] "So what you mean is that this ideal state would be ideal for the Antichrist?" commented the teacher. "But I think we're in far more danger from that famous Jewish philosopher Philo of Alexandria, who loved Plato so much that he twisted the Holy Scriptures into symbols and allegories so that the plain meaning of what God said was cancelled."

"Oh, I agree," answered the scribe, "And what if future Christian leaders used his system and ended up denying the Kingdom of God on Earth in a restored land of Israel? Hardly any unfulfilled prophecies would mean what they say." Then suddenly an alarming sound resonated in everyone's ears. "Look!" exclaimed the scribe, pointing in the distance toward the villa, "is that Aquila standing in front of the sunset, blowing a Shofar (ram's horn) in his Tallit?"

At once, all the Ethiopians grabbed their flutes and tambourines to serenade the sunset, dancing and singing and celebrating Psalm 19. "The heavens declare the glory of God, and the firmament shows His handiwork, day after day, night after night." Though blessed and enthralled by the beauty of it all, the teacher began gathering the students together with everyone else under the palm trees saying, "We've really got to go now. This means they're ready to start tonight's Revelation reading!"

The lamps were lighted and the awesome scroll was brought out. Then the aged Apostle John himself, in a wavering voice, again evoked his devastating encounter with Yeshua Messiah as the Almighty, the only ascended Master and Creator of the Universe!

> "I turned around to see who was talking with me and what I saw were seven gold lampstands and among them there was what looked like a human being, wearing a robe that reached to his feet, and a gold band around his chest. His hair was white as wool or as snow, and his eyes blazed like fire. His feet shone like brass that has been refined and polished, and his voice sounded like a roaring waterfall. He held seven stars in his right hand, and a sharp two-edged sword came out of his mouth. His face was as bright as the midday sun. When I saw him, I fell down at his feet like a dead man. He placed his right hand on me and said, "Don't be afraid! I am the First and the Last. I am the Living One! I was dead, but now I am alive forever and ever. And I hold the keys of death and Hades."[199]

For this disciple, who had been the closest intimate friend of Jesus on Earth, to be terrified at His new appearance in heaven, forced all the listeners to realize that things had drastically changed! Still visibly shaken by his overwhelming supernatural experiences, John stopped reading and motioned for Aquila to continue. Everyone in the room was riveted, no matter how many times they had heard it. Many hoped to memorize much of it and also Priscilla had set aside a special room, light and airy, for all the visiting scribes to make copies in the new codex form.

A great hush of stunned silence and awe enveloped the assembled group after hearing the whole apocalypse read. But in another, unseen dimension, the personal angels who had charge over the believers, were bestowing blessings on each of them for listening to the new book. In it, Yeshua had invoked a double blessing for the one who reads it and the one who hears it.[200] Although it was fantastically horrific, especially when matched up with the parallel predictions of the prophets, there could be no Kingdom of God coming on Earth without it all happening.

"Who would like to join me in the courtyard for a midnight question and answer time?" called out the teacher to everyone in general, but it was mostly the students who ran to get pillows and blankets. "Now," he began as they all picked grapes from the pergola; "Who would like to tell about their favorite part of the book?" As many hands went up, he pointed to the redheaded middle brother. Jumping to his feet, he shouted out "I liked the part about the two fire-breathing prophets!" "Well," said the teacher, barely concealing a laugh, "Please tell us all about it."

With wide-awake excitement he began, "Oh, I just love this part about the three superhuman characters! First, God sends down two prophets who breathe fire out of their mouths to kill their enemies. For three and a half years, they proclaim the Lord's message, while sending drought and plagues but they can't be killed by any mere mortal humans. While a new temple of God has been built in the Holy City, it is spiritually called Sodom and Egypt and the other nations have taken over a lot of it."

With red hair curling and arms gesturing, he speeded up the dramatization, "But then, Satan's superhuman beast-king rises up out of the abyss and God lets him make war on the prophets and kill them, because their assignment is finished. A great party celebration with gift giving erupts for three and a half days as the people see the dead bodies of the two tormenting prophets still lying in the street. So what does God do? He brilliantly directs an event that only He can. For maximum shock, He sends the breath of life into them. The two prophets rise from the dead before everyone's bulging eyes and, just as a commanding voice says, 'Come up here!' they rise up through the sky on a cloud as their enemies help-lessly watch.

"But a complete attitude change hits when an earthquake strikes the same hour, collapsing a tenth of the city and killing 7,000 people. All of the survivors are converted by the fear of the Lord and give glory to God.[201] Why couldn't the beast-king be killed? Remember I said that he also is super-human and Yeshua will be the only One who can destroy him.[202] But before that, a space war breaks out between the Archon Michael and his holy angels and the Dragon Satan and his fallen angels. They're defeated and thrown down to the Earth.[203] Then the Dragon possesses his underworld king, doing magic miracles and so the people worship and say, 'Who can make war with him?' Yeshua, The Lion of the Tribe of Judah, answers that question by going forth to fight, and when His feet stand on the Mount of Olives, it splits in half, moving north and south with a big earthquake."[204]

Finally, the redhead breathlessly stopped and sat down, as he saw other students waving their arms, waiting for someone else to have their turn. Unexpectedly, the teacher picked the oldest brother, saying, "We haven't seen you for a week, so what part do you choose from what you heard tonight?" Fighting off drowsiness, he stood up tall, announcing, "I like the next part so I'll just continue where my brother left off. King Messiah fights as the Avenger of the blood of his servants by trampling the enemy armies like grapes. This creates a river of blood and mud five feet deep for 200 miles and gives Jesus blood-soaked clothing.[205] As you recall, on the cross He had no garments, so His blood poured down on the land of Israel, as the Lamb of God, their Passover Lamb!"[206]

Loud applause from above caused everyone to look up at the balcony. "Please forgive me," Priscilla apologized, "But I couldn't resist interrupting your excellent performance. It connects to a mystery about the Second Coming of Christ, which I would appreciate your letting me tell you about." Having borrowed Aquila's Tallit for a shawl, she wrapped up in it against the night chill and slowly descended the stairway. "I need to remind you all that Armageddon cannot happen until AFTER the fabulous wedding feast up in the heavenly New Jerusalem. Can anyone here describe this fantastic celestial city?"

Nearly all the Ethiopian's hands went up, and their leader said, "Even though we just heard about this extra-terrestrial Jerusalem tonight, we'll never be able to forget it! It's opulent beyond belief and reminds me that our Savior has promised us rewards of gold, silver and jewels for obedience to God when He judges the quality of our works. But who could ever imagine a 1500 mile cubed space city with 12 foundations encrusted with 12 different colors of precious gems and the whole thing looking like a diamond and filled with transparent gold? Then one of their scribes added "Yes, but also there are 12 huge pearl gates guarded by 12 angels and a crystal river of life inside leading to the Throne of God and The Lamb!" "True," agreed the leaders, "and the trees of life line both banks of the river bearing 12 different kinds of fruit monthly."[207]

"You're both right," replied Priscilla. "What a supreme setting for a wedding! For the uncountable multitude of one new humanity out of every nation, language and tribe, all in their super-immortal bodies, glowing in pure white linen garments. But notice that, just to remind the world of its debt to Israel, the One who calls Himself 'The God of Israel,' and who even incarnated in Jewish flesh, has put the names of His Son's 12 Jewish apostles on the foundation gems, and the names of the 12 tribes of Israel on the pearl gates."[208]

Gasping at the unheard of magnificence they were all visualizing, everyone cheered her on to continue. "Thank you for your attentiveness since I know you all have to be sleepy by now." Then she pointed out the mystery of how Jesus could ride out of the sky after the wedding, already having bloody garments before making war at Armageddon. "Obviously, as our young friend just declared, He has to have come down much earlier, before the seven bowls of God's final wrath. In fact, that's the very reason the whole world gathers its armies, to make war on Him and us!"[209]

Waving his hand high, one of the students asked her, "How do we know that it's the Lord Jesus Himself who will do this 200 mile massacre?" She complimented him on an excellent question and responded, "That's the wonderful thing about God telling the end from the beginning. Hundreds of years ago, He gave a detailed picture of this event to Isaiah the prophet, with exact locations and quotations, all recorded with perfect precision."[210]

Turning around to walk to the balcony stairway, Priscilla paused at she put one hand on the railing. "Before I say good-night, I want to leave you with this odd story. I could never figure out how we would get back down to rule on Earth with Jesus, after He had come to take us up to our dwelling places that He had prepared in heaven. Would He give us all angel wings to fly back or what? So imagine my astonishment when John saw us all on white horses following the King of Kings on His! That will be our cosmic transportation forever! No wings needed! We'll be like clouds moving over the Earth! Hallelujah!!" One of the students sitting near the stairway asked, "Why do you suppose He chose horses instead of angel wings?" Throwing her arms up to the sky and tossing her head back in triumph, Priscilla proclaimed ecstatically, "Because He said He has made us more than conquerors and conquerors always ride white horses! That is why Yeshua the Son of the Living God will ride the greatest white horse of all! Isn't it amazing? Heaven has held this secret until now!"[212]

30
THE KINGDOM STRIKES BACK

T he next morning, quite a crowd was gathered around the villa's grand entrance, preparing their departures. As the three brothers and their pastor were readying the carriage and horses, the nine year old rummaged inside to find more fine wool gift tunics. Then Aquila invited everyone to pick figs from his trees for their trip as Priscilla was giving out holy hugs and kisses. The philosophy teacher had a final farewell message.

"Now that you know we're the cloud corps, remember that if you want to ride a white horse with the King on the clouds, you'll have to remain faithful! Whenever you're troubled, just look up at the blue sky and visualize the clouds as white horses and recall that when the Harpazo happens, we'll be snatched up in the clouds.[213] Don't forget the crown rewards you can earn in sky city and strive to be overcomers.

But if this apocalypse should come in our lifetime, the number one thing is to never ever take the 666 mark of the beastly dragon messiah of Satan–under any circumstances! Far better to starve or be tortured or killed than to burn in the lake of fire forever and ever with no escape.[214]

"However, Jesus said to pray to be counted worthy to escape all these things and to keep extra oil for your spirit-lamp and be ready to go into the wedding after hearing the shout 'Behold, the Bridegroom comes, go out to meet Him!' But then He said that half wouldn't be ready when the door was shut because He didn't know them personally in a relationship of love and obedience.[215] But be assured, I'll be praying for all of you to have tenacious patience and faith to win the victory." While waving goodbye, the teacher called out, "I'll try to visit some of your cities to bring the book of Revelation."

Rumbling along the Roman roads in their horse drawn carriage, the three brothers were feeling disappointed in the attitude of their pastor. Listening to him gossiping and complaining about the Lord's letters to the seven congregations, they began to wonder what sort of report he would give in public at their assembly. Their Pastor grumbled, "Why did Jesus have to be so hard on us?" He said Smyrna was poor but rich and we in Laodicea were rich, but really poor, blind and naked! And I couldn't believe it when He said because we were lukewarm instead of hot or cold. He was going to vomit us out of His mouth!"

Continuing in his protest, the Pastor said, "Imagine my embarrassment when all the other pastors heard that! Ephesus was complimented on their good works and correct doctrine, but Jesus warned they had lost their first love. Philadelphia got no criticism at all, but Sardis was told they were dead, even though they were thought to be alive. Do you boys remember what the problems were at the other two congregations?" Swallowing a fig he had been chewing on, the older brother answered, "Yes, I do. Actually the case in Thyatira bothered me the most even though the city of Pergamon has the altar of Zeus which Jesus called 'the throne of Satan.'"

"Can you believe in Thyatira they allow this Jezebel-type false prophetess to teach deep, secret Satanic rituals and take Christians to pagan sacrifice festivals? No wonder Jesus threatened her and her followers with death," exclaimed the middle brother. But then the nine year old couldn't contain himself any longer and just had to speak up. "Please don't feel bad, Pastor, because Yeshua even gave our congregation the greatest promise of all! That if we change and are overcomers, we will get to sit with Him on His throne! What could be more fantastic than that?"

After that, they were all mostly silent for the rest of the trip, quietly pondering these things. They concluded that many believers had forgotten that Jesus is alive and when they hear the letters, they'll really know it since He has seen and heard everything they've done and said! He also corrects

281

them because He loves them and is knocking on their doors to be opened for a dinner of close communion with Him.[216]

After bringing the boys back to their parents' house in Laodicea, the Pastor declined their dinner invitation saying he just wanted to go home and meditate until the Sabbath assembly. Then after hugs and greetings and questions about why they stayed away so long, the boys all announced to their startled parents, "We feel like we're coming back from the future!" After quizzical looks around the dinner table, the eldest son mentioned how they had been instructed by a former philosophy teacher from Athens.

Unable to resist giving a few glimpses of the new book, he began, "This teacher explained to us about the dragon kingdom that will emerge from the abyss in the end of the age. People will worship Satan, the dragon and his wicked, lawless messiah who destroys them through the deception of false peace, safety and prosperity. He will be a master of magic and sorcery who does great miracles and wonders by the empowering energy of Lucifer, who is Satan."[217]

"But just wait till you hear this whole apocalypse!" interrupted the middle redheaded brother. "About 90% of Earth's population dies or disappears into another dimension. And from God's throne in heaven, Jesus unleashes wars, cataclysms, meteors, asteroids, sun flares, volcanoes, tidal waves, earthquakes, plagues, droughts, huge hailstones, fires, floods, tornadoes, hurricanes, blood and smoke. Those are just some of His cosmic weapons to compel Earth dwellers to acknowledge God as Creator of the universe. The people flee in terror and hide in caves, trying to escape His wrath while He shakes the Earth and the mountains and islands are moving and sinking! And that's only about one third of the way through seven seals, seven trumpets and seven bowls of the Day of the Lord!"[218]

Coughing and almost choking on his food, their father protested. "The change in you boys seems extreme, I'm not sure I like it." Their mother added, "Perhaps studying that Revelation book has made you too radical for Messiah!" They retorted, "Is that worse than lukewarm?" But all three felt the Holy Spirit warning them it would be unwise to share any more details from this unique and ultimate horror book, which nevertheless promised a double blessing.

The next day, after their parents had gone to the business facility, the three brothers decided to go for a hike around the hills near the river valleys and perhaps poke around at their uncle's old house. Packing some Persian walnuts and goat cheese wrapped in grape leaves, along with bread, a knife and a clump of raisins, they set off for the day, taking the hand carved walking staffs they had made themselves. With a deep breath of freedom, they were happy that it wasn't yet time for the tutors to come for their schooling.

As they walked, it was hard now not to notice the sky since the clouds had a new secret significance. After a long hike, they climbed up on a large rocky cliff and could see the uncle's abandoned house in the distance. "Look at all the

large shade trees around it," said the eldest. "It's also covered with climbing vines and we could pretend it's our hide-
away!" The other two agreed. "We're getting hungry and we
can use it for our lunch and a rest...if it's not too scary!" As
the sun was getting hotter, they remembered to look for the
old well as they climbed down the hill toward the house.

Theirs was an ethnically blended family. Their father
was Greek and dabbled in philosophy and mythology but
mostly worshipped business, although he did believe who
Jesus is. Their mother was Jewish and followed Yeshua but
the family didn't attend all the congregation meetings. When
her brother's wife died in childbirth, he had asked them to
adopt his newborn son. That was nine years ago. As the boy
grew up he always knew he was adopted, but had been told
he was an orphan baby brought to their congregation by a
company of Jewish believers from Babylon. Supposedly
they were caring for the baby of a couple who had died from
an accident on the way.

But ever since his wife had died, the uncle lived like a
recluse, just studying his big collection of old scrolls. He
never came to family gatherings and when they sometimes
caught a distant glimpse of him in the marketplace, he was
dressed all in black with a deathly pallor. The worst thing,
however, was the rumors they heard about him betraying
believers to the enemy and stirring up pagan riots against
them, sometimes leading to execution. So it was no surprise
the previous year, when they heard a neighbor had found him

long dead in his house, therefore having him buried quickly without a rabbi doing the proper rituals.

Opening all doors and windows to air out the smell, two brothers stayed in the main room to clean out dirt and spider webs. Being curious, the youngest said he was going to search in the bedroom for keepsakes or hidden treasure. Intrigued by a small, ornate cabinet next to the bed, he began moving it away from the wall to get a closer look, when a secret compartment unlatched from the back of it, spilling out ancient parchments! Stooping over to pick them up, the young boy gasped in shock at the symbols of Kabbala and black magic. They were copies of occult secret doctrines from Babylon, with curses, spells and blasphemies on Yeshua and His mother, including slanders and plots to destroy and overthrow the body of His disciples.

After continuing to read the sickening sagas about beliefs in God having a wife and offspring of gods continually having sex along with complicated hierarchies of mediating angels, he had to call in his brothers. It didn't take long for them to be really disgusted with this discovery and said, "Let's go out to the courtyard to eat lunch and decide what to do about all this–if it hasn't ruined our appetite! Bringing some chairs and benches outdoors to dust them off, the first thing they all decided was that the Kabbala collection would have to be burned and then the house needed to be purified and exorcized!

Sticking in the knife to open one of the walnuts, the eldest said; "I think a lot of these pseudo Jews that Jesus referred to as 'The Synagogue of Satan'[219] were probably among the 95% that stayed in Babylon and picked up the mystery cults, after the first temple (of Solomon) was destroyed for their having put idols in it."[220] Then the middle brother remembered what happened in the Persian empire when Queen Esther pleaded with King Xerxes to decree that the Jews could defend themselves against the plot of Haman to have them all killed. "On the Purim holiday that celebrates their survival," he recalled, "the scroll of Esther says that many people of other nationalities became Jews because fear of the Jews had seized them."[221]

Reclining on a shaded bench with a bunch of raisins, the youngest announced, "That was hundreds of years ago. I'll bet they just mixed some old gods in with the Jew's God." Giving his brothers a knowing look, the eldest exclaimed, "That's it! The false prophet in Revelation will probably be related to those mystical mixture Kabbalists of the synagogue of Satan. This will be how he gets power to bring down fire from the sky like Elijah the ancient prophet. "Of course," replied the nine year old, "even I know that Scripture says Elijah must come first, before the Messiah. So that's how the people will be deceived–by miracles.

Standing up and stretching with a yawn, the youngest said, "This discussion is getting too deep and weird for me, I'm going to go back inside and pick up all those parchments and pile them on the bed. You look for some cords so we can tie them up for burning." "Good," agreed the other two, "but first we'll beat more dust out of these cushions with our walking staffs." Once back in the bedroom again, the nine year old realized he had forgotten to open the drawers on the front of the old cabinet. Looking in the top one, he carefully sorted through some old coins, cryptic amulets and even a small dagger.

But the bottom drawer seemed to be stuck and he had to force open what was probably a broken lock with the dagger. Then pulling out a parchment on the bottom, turned upside down under an engraved silver cup, he straightened it out on the bed to read. All of a sudden clasping one hand over his mouth to stifle a scream and grabbing his stomach with the other to stop the nausea, he stared at the adoption agreement document and couldn't believe his eyes!

Falling to the floor in a fetal position, he began rolling and moaning, "Oh No! Oh No!" he gasped over and over trying to imagine that the only parents he had ever known had lied to him! By the time his brothers had rushed in to find him, he was jumping up with a red face of fury, throwing the Kabbala parchments at the ceiling and shouting, "This black magic man, this wicked enemy of ours! This evil uncle IS MY FATHER!!!"

The boy collapsed in a sobbing heap on the bed, as the other two wept with him, trying to overcome their own shock. "We didn't know anything about this either," they cried. "Honestly, we're so sorry and confused too." Finally, they hugged and prayed and calmed him down enough to go back outdoors and drink some cool well water splashing it on their faces. "We have to talk this over and commit our future to the Lord," said the nineteen year old. "We should not let anyone know what we found out and we have to forgive everyone involved or God won't forgive us.[223] As the heir, I'll have to do more work in our family business, but it's wonderful that they gave us this summer vacation trip and we need to thank and honor our parents more according to the Lord's commandment, regardless of our emotions."[224]

Shaking his head in solemn agreement, the middle red-head then excitedly said, "But wait a minute, it just occurred to me that it was God's mercy that He rescued you from being brought up as the son of a sorcerer and gave you to his sister's family to be blessed as one of our brothers! Let's scrub and whitewash this house and overcome evil with good!"

"Great idea!" they all agreed. "Our mother would have inherited this place and we can use it in the evenings for a White Horse Force fellowship, studying this revolutionary new book with everyone who wants to come!" "Little brother," exclaimed the eldest, laying a hand on his forehead, "Apostle Peter wrote that we are a chosen generation, a royal priesthood, and a holy nation. You escaped being chosen for the troops of the Antichrist so we all should kneel and take a vow to be faithful and valiant to be chosen for the cloud cavalry of the King of Kings."[225]

Having learned some Hebrew from his tutor, the youngest asked, "Can we have as our code and password, AHAVA-AVODA? Because it means love, worship, and work, and as Rabbi Saul (Paul) wrote, 'without love we are nothing and gain nothing and it's greater than faith and hope.'"[226] "Yes, of course" replied the eldest. "He called it the more excellent way, I think, because it is the essence of God, and His cross is the eternal picture of it."

Meanwhile, the redhead had tied up the parchments for the fire. "We can't forget to burn these now and do the exorcism," he urged. Finding the necessary implements, they poured on some oil, lit it and formed a prayer circle, as the flames devoured the devil's devices. "Heavenly Father, You are our real, eternal Father, and we thank and praise You for everything! Now, as He instructed, we agree together in Jesus' Name and cancel every curse, every hex, every vex and every spell back to all generations of our family, and we break their power and cast out every demon spirit by invoking the Blood of Yeshua the Messiah!"[227]

As they sang psalms and praises to the Lord while preparing to leave, the oldest brother reminded them all, "It is written that flesh and blood cannot inherit the kingdom of God, so we will boldly go where no atheist can ever go. When we get our super-immortal bodies, it is then that the kingdom strikes back!"[228]

Conclusion

⸺꙰꙰⸺

The Truth is out there. He came down to Earth and joined the conversation! Every time people tried to delete His messages, they just multiplied because they were extra-terrestrial intelligence from a superior civilization called the Kingdom of Heaven.

Already He had sent text messages to planet Earth for thousands of years by downloading them to His true prophets through the Holy Spirit. Then finally, he showed up in Person on a love mission to make a New World Offer. It would be a promise of total transformation of spirit, soul and body as a super-immortal for anyone who believes. To prove this offer, He sealed it in blood. His own!

Of course, no man could ever become God. But God could, and did, become a Man. Why? To seed a supernatural race of imitators and overcomers trained to reign with Him when He returns as the only rightful heir of the Global

Throne. Maybe you've never met Him because you never asked. So quiet down and say something like this:

"If there really is a God out there, please let me know. If Your Book is for real, please help me understand it."

So, opt out of the New World Order and go for the New World Offer!

ENDNOTES

1— Isaiah 14:12-14

2— Ezekiel 28:13-17

3— Ephesians 6:12

4— Ezekiel 28:12

5— Isaiah 14:15

6— Revelation 4:11 King James Version

7— Matthew 25:41

8— Matthew 12:26

9— Daniel 7:9-10

10— Ezekiel 28:12

11— Job 38: 4-7

12— Genesis 1:1-25

13— Genesis 1:26-27

14— Genesis 1:28-31

15— Genesis 2:18-25

16— Genesis 3:1-5

17— Genesis 3:6-20

18— Genesis 3:21-24

19— Genesis 6:1-4

20— Genesis 6:5-10

21— Genesis 6:11-22

22— Genesis 7:1-24

23— Genesis 8:1-22

24— Genesis 9:1-17

25— Genesis 10:8-12

26— Genesis 11:1-4

27— Genesis 11:5-9

28— Hebrews 11:8

29— Genesis 12:1-7

30— Genesis 9:18-29

31— Genesis 17:15-22, 18:10-15

32— Genesis 18:16-33

33— Genesis 19:1-29

34— Genesis 23:1-20

35— Genesis 24:1-67

36— Genesis 25:20-26

37— Genesis 32:6-7

38— Genesis 25:27-34, 27:1-46

39— Genesis 32:24-32

40— Genesis 33:1-20

41— Genesis 46:1-27

42— Exodus 1:1-22

43— Exodus 3:1-22, 4:1-17

44— Exodus 4:21-23, Chapter 7-12

45— Exodus 13:20-22

46— Exodus Chapters 14&15

47— Luke 1:26-38, Matthew 1:18-25

48— Genesis 3:14-15

49— Philippians 2:5-11

50— Isaiah 7:14, Matthew 1:23

51— Isaiah 9:6-7

52— Luke 2:1-7

53— Leviticus 23:33-43

54— Luke 2:1-7

55— Malachi 4:2

56— Matthew 2:1-23, Micah 5:1-2

57— Luke 2:41-52

58— Luke 1:5-25, 36-80, John 1:29-34, Matthew 3:13-17

59— Matthew 4:1-11, Luke 4:1-14

60— Mark 2:13-17

61— John 3:22-30

62— Matthew 14:1-12, 11;1-14

63— Matthew 14:14-21, Luke 8:1-15

64— Mark 1:23-25, Matthew 8:29

65— John 8:42-47

66— John 12:43, Matthew 21:31

67— John 3:1-19, 36

68— Matthew 6:28-33, 19-21

69— Matthew 18:1-16, 19:13-14

70— Matthew 7:28-29, Mark 7:6-9&13

71— Matthew 11:28-30 5:11-12, 43-44

72— Luke 10:1-18, John 10:10

73— Luke 10:38-42

74— Mark 3:20-21 & 31-34

75— Hebrews 3:1-6, Matthew 10:34-38, John 16:33

76— John 11:1-48

77— Matthew 11:18-19 & 9:14-15

78— Luke 17:20-25

79— Luke 4:16-30

80— Zechariah 9:9, Matthew 21:4-5

81— John 2:13-17, Mark 11:15-18

82— Revelation 12:9, Luke 8:26-39

83— John 10:17-18

84— John 6:70, Mark 3:17

85— Luke 22:14-20

86— Isaiah 42:6, John 14:2,3,6

87— John 13:4-8

88— Matthew 26:14-23, Zechariah 11:12-13

89— Luke 22:40-46

90— John 3:14-15, Numbers 21:8-9

91— Isaiah 53:7-10, Philippians 2:6-8

92— Luke 22:47-48, Matthew 26:63-68, Daniel 7:13-14

93— Matthew 27:19

94— John 18:31-32, Acts 6:12-15;54-59

95— Isaiah 53:5

96— Isaiah 52:13-14

97— John 19:1-24

98— Matthew 26:53-54, Luke 23:32-34

99— Psalm 22:1-18 Matthew 27:46

100— Hebrews 12:2, Revelation 7:9, 19:6-9, Isaiah 53.10

101— John 19:25-36, Luke 23:44-49

102— Numbers 9:12, Psalm 34:20, John 19:38-42

103— 2 Peter 2:4, Jude 6. 1 Timothy 3:6, Genesis 6, Revelation 1:18 & 9:11, Philippians 2:9-11

104— Matthew 25:41, Ephesians 6:12, Colossians 2:15, James 2:19, Psalm 14:1

105— Luke 16:22-26, John 19:25-27

106— Luke 24:1-12, John 20:10-17

107— Matthew 28:2-4, 7:52-53

108— John 20:19-21, Luke 24:9-12

109— Luke 24:36-44

110— Matthew 19:28-29

111— John 21:1-19

112— Matthew 28:18-20, Mark 16:15-19

113— Isaiah 2:1-4, Ch. 60, Matthew 10:6, John 10:14 16

114— Acts 1:6-9, Luke 24:47-52

115— Acts 1:10-13, John 14:1-3

116— Matthew 27:62-66

117— Acts 2:1-24, 36-40, Proverbs 30:4, Joel 2:28-32

118— Exodus 32:1-29, Acts Chapter 3 & 4 1:4

119— Acts 2:42-47 & 5:12-42

120— Acts 2:1-25, Galatians 1:11-24

121— Acts 10:1-48 & 11:1-18

122— Matthew 26:26-29

123— Matthew 22:1-3, Revelation 19:7-9, 1 Peter 1:18-19, Isaiah 43:10-11

124— Matthew 7:21-23

125— Galatians 2:11-21

126— John 7:2-5, Numbers 15:37-40

127— Acts 15:1-31

128— 2 Corinthians 4:4 & 2:11 & 11:13-51

129— Isaiah 5:20, 1 Timothy 4:1

130— Acts 17:6-7

131— Acts 18:1-4&7-11

132 - Genesis 2:2 & Exodus 20:8-11

133— 1 Corinthians 6:9-11

134— Luke 7:37-47 & 12-7 & Revelation 4:11 (KJV)

135— 1 Corinthians 13:1 & 14:2

136— Herbrews 9:25-27

137— 1 Thessalonians 4:13-18, Phlippians 3:20-21 & John 4:22

138— Psalm 68:11 (in various translations)

139— Matthew 9:20 & 14:36

140— Judges 6:25

141— Matthew 10:36-39 & 5:43-44 & 6:14-15

142— John 8:31-32, 34-36

143— Psalm 16:11

144- Zephaniah 2:11

145— Romans 8:18-23

146— Isaiah 11:6-9

147— Acts 16:11-15,40

148— Isaiah 2:6-22

149— Matthew 25:31-32 & 40-46, Matthew 10:42

150— John 17:5 & Ezekiel 10:1 & 1:26; Matthew 28:18
& Acts 17:30-31; Luke 21:22; Luke 19:12,14,27 &
Matthew 22:6-7

151— Hebrews 6:18, Jeremiah 32:28-29, Isaiah 45:1,
Daniel 9:26, Matthew 23:37-39

152— Isaiah 14:12-15, Ezekiel 28:11-17 & Genesis 6:1-8

153— 1 Peter 4:12-13

154— 2 Corinthians 11:23-28, Acts 16:16-40

155— Philippians 1:21

156— Luke 7:1-6

157— Leviticis 23:34&39-43

158— Zechariah 14:16-19 & Isaiah 7:14 & Matthew
1:22-23

159— Mark 13:1-2

160— Daniel 9:26 Zechariah 14:9 & Jeremiah 3:17

161— 1 Thessalonians 4:15-17

162— Matthew 24:44&48-51

163— 1 Corinthians 6:2

164— Acts 17:16-34

165— Jeremiah 7:18

166— Revelation 17&18

167— John 16:14

168— 1 Timothy 2:5& Acts 4:12

169— Revelation 13&17

170— Isaiah 31:8 & Daniel 8:25

171— Leviticus 18:22 & Romans 1:27, 32

172— 2 Timothy 2:12

173— Hebrews 10-34 & Matthew 5:5

174— Mark 16:17-18

175— Colossians 3:2

176— Hebrews 10:34

177— Revelation 2:8-11

178— Micah 5:5-6, Isaiah 14:25

179— Daniel 9:26-27

180— Revelation 9:14-21

181— Revelation 9:1-11

182— Romans 1:27

183— 1 John 1:9

184— Genesis 6:1-5

185— Genesis 1:27-28

186— Jeremiah 7:30-31, Ezekiel 23;37-39

187— Luke 17:26-37

188— Revelation 11:8

189— Ezekiel 16:47-52

190— Ezekiel 16:53-63 (See website for "Tall Al Hammam" Archaelolgical dig in Jordan)

191— Matthew 11:23-24

192— Isaiah 3:9-NIV & Jeremiah 6:15-8:12

193— Acts 3:21

194— Hebrews 13:5

195— Galatians 5:22-24

196— 2 Corinthians 1:22 & Ephesians 1:13

197— 1 Peter 1:23

198— Search "Socrates Dialogue with Timmaeus on the Ideal State" and Plato's Republic

199— Revelation 1:12-18

200— Revelation 1:3

201— Revelation Chapter 11

202— Revelation 19:19-21, 2 Thessalonians 2:8, Daniel 8:25, Isaiah 31:8

203— Revelation 12:7-9

204— Revelation 13:2-4, Revelation 5:5, Zechariah 14:3-4

205— Isaiah 63:3-4, Revelation 14:3-4

206— Psalm 22:16-18, 1 Peter 1:18-19

207— 1 Corinthians 3:12-15, Revelation Chapter 21

208— Revelation 7:9-10 & 19:7-9 & 22:13,16

209— Revelation 19:13& 11:15 & 17:14&19:19

210— Isaiah Chapter 63

211— John 14, Revelation 19:14

212— Isaiah 60:8, Romans 8:37, Revelation 19:11-16

213— 1 Thessalonians 4:16-17

214— Revelation 14:9-12

215— Luke 21:35-36, Revelation 3:10 & Matthew 25:1-13

216— Revelation Chapters 2&3

217— Revelation 17:8 & 11:7 & Chapter 13 & Daniel 8:23-25

218— Revelation Chapter 6

219— Revelation 2:9&3:9

220— Ezekiel Chapters 8&9

221— Esther 8:17

222— Revelation 13:11-14, 2 Kings 1:10-12 & Malachi 4:5

223— Matthew 6:14

224— Ephesians 6:1

225— 1 Peter 2:9-10 NKJV, Matthew 24:30

226— 1 Corinthians 12:31 & 13:1-13& 1 John 4:8 & John 3:16-19

227— Matthew 18:18-20; 2 Corinthians 2:11

228—1 Corinthians 15:50-54; Revelation 2:26-28

BIBLIOGRAPHY

Aleorn, Randy. <u>Heaven</u>. Carol Stream, Illinois-Tyndale House Publishers, 2004

Barclay, William. <u>Letters To The Seven Churches</u>.Louisville, KY Westminster. John Knox Press, 1982

Church, J.R. <u>Guardians of the Grail</u>. Oklahoma City, OK. Prophecy Publications, 1989

Cooper, Bill. <u>After the Flood</u>. Chichester, England. New Wine Press, 1995

Franz, Norm. <u>Money & Wealth in the New Millennium.</u> Whitestone Press 2001

Fructenbaum, Arnold G. <u>The Footstops of the Messiah</u>. Ariel Ministries, 1982

Heidler, Robert D. <u>The Messianic Church</u>. Denton, TX 2000

Heron, Patrick. <u>The Nephilim and The Pyramid of The Apocalypse</u>.Xulon Press, 2005

Hislop, Alexander. <u>The Two Babylons.</u> Neptune, NJ. Loiz eaux Brothers, 1943

Kah, Gary. The New World Religion. Noblesville, Ind. Hope International Publishing, 1998

Hunt, Dave. A Woman Rides the Beast. Eugene, OR. Harvest House, 1994

Lambert Lance. Battle for Israel. Kingsway Publications. England, 1975

Lindsey, Hal. The Rapture. New York, NY. Bantam Books 1983

McBirnie, William Steuart. The Search for the Twelve Apostles. Carol Stream, Il. Tyndale House, 1973

McManners, John (ED.) Oxford Illustrated History of Christianity. Oxford, England. Oxford University Press, 1992

Powers, Kimberly. Escaping The Vampire. Colorado Springs, CO. David Cook, 2009

Quale, Stephen, Giants, Bozeman MT. End Time Publishers, 2002

Readers Digest. Great People of the Bible and How They Lived. Pleasantville, NY 1974

Unger, Merrill. Unger's Bible Dictionary. Chicago, IL. Moody Bible Institute, 1974

ABOUT THE AUTHOR

_⟨∘⟩_

Although having a college degree in Fine Arts, M.A. Meehan later became captivated by Bible prophecy, eventually realizing the need to make it understandable for all ages of readers.

The result is this "creative non-fiction" book using some real and some imaginary characters in a short story collection format.

Please enjoy and be enlightened!

CPSIA information can be obtained at www.ICGtesting.com
Printed in the USA
BVOW05s0147040814

361396BV00001B/37/P